THE

GOOD
LUCK

BOOK

THE
GOOD
LUCK
BOOK

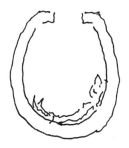

by Stefan Bechtel & Laurence Roy Stains
Illustrated by R.O. Blechman

WORKMAN PUBLISHING • NEW YORK

Library of Congress Cataloging-in-Publication Data

Bechtel, Stefan
The good luck book / by Stefan Bechtel and Laurence R. Stains;
illustrations by R.O. Blechman.
p. cm.
ISBN 0-7611-0541-7
1. Fortune—literary collections. I. Stains, Larry. II. Title.
PN6071.F66B43 1997
123'.3—dc21   97-4102
                                                               CIP

Design by Lisa Hollander and Lori S. Malkin

Workman books are available at special discounts when purchased in
bulk for premiums and sales promotions as well as for fund-raising or
educational use. Special editions or book excerpts can also be created
to specification. For details, contact the Special Sales Director at the
address below.

Workman Publishing Company
708 Broadway
New York, NY 10003-9555

Manufactured in the United States of America

First printing February 1997
10 9 8 7 6 5 4 3 2

To my beloved punks, Adam and Lilly, who make me feel like the luckiest man alive.

—*S.B.*

To Carly. Yes, we are lucky.

—*L.S.*

Acknowledgments

We have been lucky enough to receive tips and suggestions from many people during the year that we worked on this book. In particular, we'd like to extend our thanks to Denise Dugan, Pam Emory, Nichelle Gainer, Doug Jack, Carol Saline, Don Steinberg, Stuart Vyse, and Marge Dewey at the Ralph W. Miller Golf Library. And especially to Kay Bechtel, who first said "hmmm," and got us started.

Hats off to our editor, Lynn Brunelle, for her care, her judgment, and her charming manner. And to our agent, Connie Clausen, for her wisdom, her candor—and her literary luck.

Credits

For permission to use copyrighted or protected material, we thank the following literary executors and publishers. We have made every effort to obtain permission to reprint material in this book and to publish proper acknowledgments. We regret any errors or oversights.

P. 54: *Fowl Tips* by Wade Boggs. Copyright © 1997 by Wade Boggs. Reprinted by arrangement with Wade Boggs and Coordinated Sports Management Group, Inc.

P. 328: *Believing in Magic: The Psychology of Superstition* by Stuart A. Vyse. Copyright © 1997 by Stuart A. Vyse. Reprinted by arrangement with Oxford University Press.

Introduction

One of our favorite movies is *Nobody's Fool.* Paul Newman plays the character Sully, a 60-year-old construction worker who didn't build much of a life for himself. Bruce Willis plays Carl Roebuck, a guy who inherits his father's construction company, marries the prettiest woman in town—and wins most of the poker games down at the Iron Horse Bar. One night, with Sully losing as usual, it's Carl's turn to deal. Sully, sitting to his right, cuts the cards with a good-luck ritual: he makes a magic circle over the deck with his hand and then raps it with his knuckles as he utters a salty charm.

Carl looks at him. "You know, Sully, you're the only guy I know still dumb enough to believe in luck."

Why is it that the people who come down hardest on luck are usually the ones who've already gotten theirs? Sully doesn't miss a beat: "I used to believe in brains and hard work till I met you."

Like Sully, we're dumb enough to believe in luck. A couple of baby boomers now hitting midlife, we grew up thinking that life would be a tidy series of merit badges. But life is anything but tidy. There are times when everything goes right as rain. Then one day, just as mysteriously, one's luck changes and it's gone. Sound familiar?

Everyone has to take responsibility for

one's life, but that doesn't mean it's within one's control. For someone to think he or she is in charge around here is pure arrogance—the arrogance of a Carl Roebuck. Accepting the role of luck (or fate, or chance, or destiny, or Providence, or whatever you want to call it) is a sign of humility. Is it really so smart to think you call all the shots? Is Sully so dumb, after all?

In researching this book, we took a keen interest in luck as viewed by people in other places and in other times. And guess what: Sully has plenty of company. Throughout history, the greatest leaders have courted it; philosophers have pondered it; ordinary people have engaged in an infinite variety of charms and rituals in order to avoid bad luck and attract good luck.

The ancient Egyptians divided their calendar into lucky and unlucky days. Ancient Romans worshipped Fortuna, the goddess of luck. Not only did people wear their own personal good-luck charms (which is the origin of jewelry, by the way), but entire cities used to have good-luck charms—carefully hidden, of course, to keep their enemies from stealing their communal good luck.

The origin of Jewelery

In short, belief in luck is universal. So is the belief that, aside from the few people who seem to be born lucky, good luck pretty much comes and goes. Nobody should count on having good luck next week ("Luck is always borrowed, not owned," say the Norwegians), and, by the same token, bad luck is bound to change ("Behind bad luck comes good luck," say the Gypsies). Since just about forever, people have wanted to know how you keep good luck flowing when you've found it, and how to get it back when you've lost it. Luck is an enduring (and maddening!) mystery.

That's what this book is all about.

As you turn these pages, you'll see how the world pays homage to luck. We hope you'll take delight in reading about old folklore. We hope you'll be equally delighted by the charms and rituals of modern sports heroes and movie stars. For them, good-luck charms and rituals are powerful tools to keep themselves centered, focused, and "on task." Luck is useful to their success. And luck is useful, as well, to success in business. Many a self-made man or woman won't say so publicly. But as you'll see, some of America's prominent billionaires acknowledge its starring role.

We wouldn't be at all surprised if, in reading this book, you also feel like these prominent people are sharing a secret with

you. For most Americans, luck is personal.
Oh, they believe in luck, and do whatever
they can to attract it. (Nearly three out of
four adults have at least one good-luck
charm.) But most Americans keep quiet
about it. They're a little embarrassed . . . a
little conflicted. Small wonder. Americans
are supposed to succeed by pluck, not luck.
Yet every year Americans spend a third of a
trillion dollars on bingo, slot machines,
horse races, office betting pools, video
poker, and lottery tickets.

   In modern America, luck gets a bad rap.
Partly that's because some people come to
ruin by relying on it too much. (An old, old
mortal flaw!) Also it's because luck is sur-
rounded by superstition. When taken too literally, superstition can be a snare and a
delusion—you don't need a lecture about
that. If luck really could be manipulated, it
wouldn't be luck.

But we want to share some of the old folklore with you because, when taken figuratively, there's a poetry about it. To catch a falling leaf, to count the spots on a ladybug, to hold a silver coin in your hand while making a wish under the new moon—that's performance poetry. Those old rituals have all the simple beauty of folk art.

We think a good-luck charm is a way of asking fate for a favor. You may scorn the whole idea, or clasp one in earnest, or carry several with humor and a feeling that "it can't hurt." Great. Just don't make Carl Roebuck's mistake: Don't confuse superstition with luck itself. Luck is real. Luck is undeniable. Luck is out there, waiting.

You know what happens when a whole lot of good luck comes together? When it really comes along, you're "hot," and there's a kind of raw magical energy that comes with it, so much so that people want to be near

you. After all, it just might rub off! Well,
that's exactly what we hope to have done
here. We wanted to create a good-luck
charm between two covers. We've tried to
collect enough good luck in one spot to lift
your heart, boost your spirits, and raise your
hopes. With any luck, it will rub off on you. If
good luck can be given away, this book will
do the trick.

"Luck affects every-thing. Let your hook always be cast in the stream. When you least expect it, there will be fish."

—*Ovid, 1st century* A.D.

"Hap and Mishap Govern the World."

—*old English proverb*

HAP   MISHAP

Happiness Is Good Luck

The root of "happiness" is "hap"—an odd, ancient little word which means chance or luck. You can see this meaning in words like "haphazard" (aimless or determined by chance) or even "happen" (something that occurs by chance or without planning). A long time ago, a person's luck (good or bad) used to be referred to as one's "hap."

In a word, the link between happiness and good luck is built right into our language.

Cross Your Fingers

"Keep your fingers crossed for me!" is tantamount to saying, "Wish me luck!" It's also done by oneself when someone is about to receive good luck or begin a new venture. One plausible explanation is that the cross is an old and universal symbol for unity, and where two straight lines (or fingers) meet, the wish is held there until realized in fact.

In European and American folklore, people cross their fingers for other reasons as well. You're supposed to keep your fingers crossed whenever passing by a graveyard as a protection against evil spirits. And children still cross fingers while lying to "cross out" the lie, which comes from the belief that, if you at least crossed your fingers while lying, the Devil couldn't take your soul, right then and there, in its moment of sin.

There's some of that self-protective instinct at play when we cross our fingers for good luck. It "crosses out" the possibility that bad luck will dash our hopes. Maybe it will foil the malevolent spirits, who, upon hearing of our good luck, would like nothing better than to undo it.

Time-Honored Ways to Improve Your Luck

1. Catch a falling leaf and keep it.

2. Put a penny from your birth year in your penny loafers.

3. Look at the new moon while holding silver coins in your hand.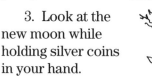

4. Catch the bubbles atop your coffee or tea with a spoon and drink them before they break.

5. Spit at a white horse.

6. Tie a string in a circle and keep it in your purse.

7. Sit with your legs crossed.

"Everything that happened to me happened by mistake. I don't believe in fate. It's luck, timing, and accident."

—*Merv Griffin*

You: A Hundred-Million-to-One Shot

If you don't believe that luck plays any role in your life, consider the incredible lottery that you won at the moment of your conception.

At that moment, a single egg produced by your mother was ready and waiting to be fertilized. Your father, by contrast, had produced a snowstorm of sperm cells, each seeking to become the lucky one to reach the target and create you. The number of spermy contenders for the job is mind-numbing—researchers say that every time a man's heart beats, his body produces roughly 1,000 new sperm cells; a single ejaculation may contain as many as 100 million.

But here's where luck comes in: Those sperm cells are not all alike. In fact, a healthy man will produce sperm that may contain tens of thousands of different variations on the basic genetic blueprint contained in his body. That's why two siblings may look so different, even though they have the same parents. That's the basis of diversity in every species.

Something or other—fate, luck, God, Providence, or some other force we know not of—chose only one of that great swarm of sperm to fertilize your mother's egg, thus creating the unique being that is you. Had a different sperm cell found the target, the you that is you would never have been created.

As French mathematician Henri Poincaré once marveled about this Lotto of the womb: "It would have sufficed to deflect [the sperm cell] a fraction of an inch, and Napoleon would not have been conceived, and the destinies of a continent would have been changed."

"The force of chance is diffused throughout the whole order of things."

—*St. Augustine*

"I firmly believe that history is chance, just like evolution. It's not the survival of the fittest, it's survival of the luckiest."

—*Stephen Ambrose, historian*

"Fate laughs at probabilities."

—*Edward Bulwer-Lytton,*
Victorian novelist

The Daruma Doll

A common good-luck charm in Japan is the daruma doll. It's named after a sixth-century A.D. Buddhist monk who, according to legend, sat so long in meditation that his arms and legs disappeared! That's what this doll looks like—an egg-shaped fellow with a rounded, heavy bottom. When you knock him over, he pops back up again. Because he recovers from every blow, he's a perfect symbol for good luck and success. And that's what the daruma doll has come to represent.

The Japanese buy a daruma before starting a new venture. It comes with both eyes painted white only—no pupils. Let's say you're taking a new job or opening a store; you'd paint a pupil on one eye and make a wish. If the wish comes true, you'd paint in the other eye as a sign of thanks.

"I knew what to do with the luck, that's the difference. Some people don't know what to do with it. I recognize an opportunity. But I never envisioned anything as huge as this."

—*Ann Landers [Eppie Lederer]*

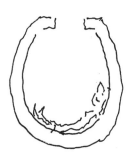

"You know what luck is? Luck is believing you're lucky . . . to hold front position in this rat-race you've got to believe you're lucky."

—*Stanley Kowalski,*
A Streetcar Named Desire

Good Advice about Good Luck

"What you may say is: 'Johnny, you may be the luckiest golfer in the world, but I am the unluckiest. Why shouldn't I get a break now and then?'

"The only answer I can give you is advice to start thinking that you are a lucky golfer. Your luck may be just the same as it has been in the game, but by feeling you have some luck you'll take a lot of pressure off yourself. It's tensity and pressure that keep most golfers many strokes higher than their game normally should be.

"I've got a notion that almost every leading golfer has some club or action or item of apparel that he deeply believes is good luck for him, even though he may keep the matter a dark secret.

"Hypnotize yourself, if you have to, into the conviction that you're lucky."

—Johnny Revolta,
1935 PGA champ

Beginner's Luck

You've probably seen or experienced it yourself: A complete and utter novice, a rank greenhorn, tries a game for the first time and has amazingly good luck. Could be gin rummy, could be Scrabble, could be pitching horseshoes. But it seems to happen so often that people simply call it "beginner's luck."

Makes you wonder if there really is anything to it.

A lot of "pros" think so. In the book *Fate, Coincidence and the Outcome of Horse Races*, author Armando Benitez, a 40-year veteran of betting at the track, admits that he's tried all manner of methods to pick a winner—including some pretty wacky ones. He's simply picked a horse's name out of a hat. He's tried paying close attention to meaningful coincidences. (He'd meet a woman named Sophie, for instance, and the next day bet on a horse named Sophie's Choice.) Not surprisingly, these methods didn't work all that well.

But he did discover a simple method that seemed to consistently improve his chances: He'd just take a complete novice to the track (usually a woman), and put his money on the horses she picked. It didn't always work. But, he confessed, it's amazing how often it did.

Maybe it's simply that the Fates smile on the innocent.

Or maybe it's just "beginner's luck."

Talismans of Tennis

❖ Boris Becker wears the same shirt he wore when he won a previous tournament.

❖ John McEnroe never stepped on the white line during play. He hated playing on any Thursday the 12th.

❖ Björn Borg would stop shaving four days before a tournament. He'd pack his tennis bag meticulously, his ten racquets stacked in descending order of tension. His mother, Margarethe, would suck hard candy while watching his final set.

❖ Billie Jean King had a lucky bathtub whenever she played Wimbledon.

❖ Martina Navratilova knocked on her racquet before she played.

❖ Mary Pierce loves the number 13. In her first national tournament, she beat the top-seeded player on Court 13.

"Yes, I believe in luck and fate. It seems that everything has been written for me . . . so I'm just going with it. That notion keeps me somewhat relaxed."

—*Teri Garr*

Some Pig

Mike Rieke is a Minnesota farmer and the proud owner of 2,000 hogs. One fine spring day in 1996 he was bending over his hogs' water trough—and a pig pulled his wallet right out of his back pocket.

Rieke had never seen anything like it. This pig danced and pranced all around the barn with the wallet in its mouth. When Rieke finally caught up with it, the first thing he did was give this smarty-pants hog a kick in the bacon.

The second thing he did was open his wallet and pull out his wad of lottery-ticket stubs. He hadn't checked to see if any were winners in quite a while.

As it turned out, Rieke was the proud owner of a winning $100,000 Powerball ticket.

He couldn't take back the kick—but he could pay for a new hog barn. And a family vacation. Meanwhile, there's one pig who won't be going to hog heaven anytime soon.

"There is a tide in the affairs
    of men
Which, taken at the flood, leads
    on to fortune;
Omitted, all the voyage of their
    life
Is bound in shallows and in
    miseries."

—*Shakespeare,* Julius Caesar

According to an old tradition, if you find your initials in a spider's web, you'll have good luck forever.

"The very best thing in all this world that can befall a man is to be born lucky."

—*Mark Twain [Samuel Clemens]*

Your Lucky Number

If the date of your birth can be added up and then divided by seven—say, 8/6/56 (8 + 6 + 56 = 70)—you'll be lucky all your life.

The *Nefer*

The written language of the ancient Egyptians was composed of symbols, or picture words, called hieroglyphs. They were like our words in that they were signs for specific sounds, but they were also symbols that could confer their meaning upon the wearer. Among the hieroglyphs, the Egyptians got a lot of use out of the term *nefer.* Over the many centuries of ancient Egyptian civilization (which arose more than 5,000 years ago) the *nefer* acquired a dozen different meanings, all positive. Used as a symbol, it meant "goodness," "beauty," "happiness," "youth"—and "good luck." Small red semiprecious stones were carved in the shape of a *nefer,* strung on necklaces, and worn as amulets. It was also carved as a repetitive image, such as the row upon row of *nefers* that graced the wide collars of young queens.

We know, from ancient papyri, that every day of the Egyptian year was divided into three parts, and each of these three parts was marked down as being either lucky or unlucky. Much like our modern daily astrology guides, it gave guidance as to good and bad times to begin ventures, for example. On those calendars, the symbol used to denote lucky days was the *nefer.*

Luckiest Days of the Year

JANUARY	JULY
4, 19, 27, 31	2, 6, 10, 23, 30
FEBRUARY	**AUGUST**
7, 8, 18	5, 7, 10, 14, 19
MARCH	**SEPTEMBER**
3, 9, 12, 14, 16	6, 10, 15, 18, 30
APRIL	**OCTOBER**
5, 27	13, 16, 20, 31
MAY	**NOVEMBER**
1, 2, 4, 6, 9, 14	3, 13, 23, 30
JUNE	**DECEMBER**
3, 5, 7, 9, 12, 23	10, 20, 29

—Zolar's Encyclopedia of Signs,
Omens, and Superstitions

"A man likes to feel he's in control of his life, but it's a damned illusion. The X factor is always there. You can have all the talent in the world, but

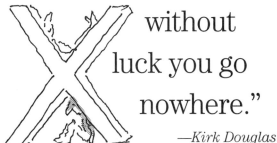 without luck you go nowhere."

—*Kirk Douglas*

Your Lucky Star

People everywhere have gazed in wonder at the starry, starry night. They have believed that all those breathtaking stars are gods or fallen heroes, and that they have unseen influence over our affairs way down here.

From the ancient belief that the stars guide our destinies comes the idea of a guiding star for each and every person, which appears at our birth and disappears at our demise. It waxes and wanes, rises and falls, directing our lot in life. Napoleon was convinced he had a "star of destiny"; so was Hitler. The saying that someone is "a rising star" has its origin in this belief. So does the notion that someone has a lucky star. Today it's a way of showing humility and saying, in effect, "I've been blessed." Newscaster Katie Couric, for example, likes to say she was born under a lucky star; we doubt she thinks there's really a star up there somewhere with her name on it.

The link between luck and the stars is also expressed in the Hebrew phrase *mazel tov*, which is generally taken to mean "good luck." Actually, it is something closer to "good constellation" or "may the stars be good to you." The basic idea is that, whatever the occasion, you're wishing it will be blessed by a favorable arrangement of the stars.

"God made the heavens, and Luck makes the Stars!"

—*old Broadway saying*

Shooting Stars

Falling stars are especially lucky for lovers, provided they wish together when they see one. Shooting stars are lucky, as well, for sick people (they'll regain their health within thirty days) and travelers (it's an omen of a successful trip).

Are you especially silver-tongued? If you can say "money-money-money" before it vanishes from sight, you'll be prosperous.

In all these cases, the wish must be made quickly or it won't come true.

Star light, star bright
First star I see tonight;
I wish I may, I wish
    I might
have the wish I wish
    tonight.

           —traditional English rhyme

"Whenever you can, hang around the lucky."

—*Jewish saying*

Fore!

The hole-in-one is that instant when good luck meets the game of golf. When it happens—and it has happened to tens of thousands of people—it's more than a milestone. It becomes a defining moment in life.

The hole-in-one is usually viewed as a combination of luck and skill. If it were pure luck, then the odds would favor amateurs more than they do. As it is, a male professional's or top amateur golfer's chances of hitting a hole in one are 3,708 to 1; a female pro's odds are 4,648 to 1. The average duffer's chances are 42,952 to 1. In other words, you're four times likelier to be hit by a car.

And yet if it were merely skill, then it wouldn't happen for a six-year-old girl. Or a blind man. Or a man playing his very first game of golf. (Okay, so he teed off from the ninth hole—and landed in the 13th.) Or a woman playing her first hole. But it did happen to all these people. It happens to people twice in the same round of golf—all the time, actually. It's happened to people playing on three consecutive days, and to two people playing the same hole. Here's the all-time coincidence: In 1989, four players in the U.S. Open in Rochester, New York, all aced the same hole during the same round. Talk about beating the odds—somebody figured it at 1.89 quadrillion to one.

If a hole-in-one were merely skill, then pure persistence ought to do the trick. But it doesn't. One time, in 1940, a golfer stepped up to the tee and proceeded to whack 1,817 balls at a flag 160 yards away. Sixteen hours and 25 minutes later, he gave up and went home. Later, a Massachusetts fellow tried even harder, and took 3,333 whacks. Zip. Nada. Not a one.

And yet . . . In 1981, a 17-year-old

Englishman was clowning around one day;
he stepped up to the tee of a 174-yard hole
with his putter. The resulting shot resembled
a line drive—but it dropped right into the
cup. In 1959, another Englishman without an
ace to his name hit his ball with a five-iron.
The ball took a sharp left turn, bounced off a
drainage pipe to the left of the fairway,
skipped across the grass to a greenside
bunker, hit a rake, popped onto the green,
glanced off the ball of a fellow player—and
rolled into the hole for an ace.

    Now that's good luck—even if he was ex-
pected to buy drinks for everyone in the
clubhouse afterward.

"We must believe in luck. For how else can we explain the success of those we don't like?"

—*Jean Cocteau*

Play Ball! But First . . .

Ever since baseball was invented, there have been baseball players in need of good luck. They have worked hard to get it in many ways: following an identical course to the bench; touching second base on the way to the outfield; spitting on their gloves; not walking between the ump and the catcher; not stepping on chalk lines; not washing their socks; not having the first guy at bat foul out.

Today's players continue to be mindful of their rituals. For instance:

✤ California Angels reliever Mike James must use the same hair gel, doesn't wash his stirrup socks, and doesn't want anyone trying on his glove. During warmup, he won't pick up the baseball if it's rolling.

✤ Seattle Mariners pitcher Randy Johnson eats pancakes before his starts at home.

He also tries to play his drums that day—
to help him relax, he says.

✣ Chicago Cubs pitcher Turk Wendell has
   eased up a bit from his minor-league days,
   when he brushed his teeth in the dugout
   between innings. Then he would jump over
   the foul line on the way to the mound
   while pointing at the center fielder. Once
   on the mound, he ate black licorice.

An All-Star List of Sports Charms

1. Michael Jordan wears his old college basketball shorts underneath his Chicago Bulls uniform.

2. San Francisco 49ers coach George Seifert blows three times through the hole of a Life-Saver before popping it in his mouth.

3. Hockey legend Wayne Gretzky tucks in only the right side of his jersey.

4. Auto racer Mario Andretti refused to sign autographs with a green pen.

5. Hank Aaron wore the same pair of shower shoes for 20 years.

6. Larry Bird always rubbed his hands on his sneakers before going onto the court.

7. Wilt Chamberlain always wore a rubber band on his right wrist.

8. Tennis star Jimmy Connors carried a note from his grandmother inside his sock.

9. Track star Jackie Joyner-Kersee has to eat chicken before every meet.

10. When sports announcer John Madden coached the Oakland Raiders, nobody could leave the locker room until running back Mark van Eeghen had burped.

Lucky Lemon Chicken

Wade Boggs has eaten chicken before every baseball game since 1982, when he went five for six against the Cardinals in spring training after a chicken dinner. When it comes to poultry dishes, he's tried 'em all. Here's a meal from his cookbook of favorite chicken recipes, *Fowl Tips:*

> *2 to 3 pounds chicken (cut up)*
> *garlic salt to taste*
> *1 stick butter*
> *2 teaspoons dry mustard*
> *1½ to 2 cups lemon juice*

1. Preheat oven to 400°F. Rinse chicken and pat dry. Sprinkle chicken pieces with garlic salt and place in shallow baking pan.

2. In a sauce pan, melt butter. Add dry mustard and lemon juice and baste chicken pieces. Bake for 1 hour, basting often.

"In the past, eating lemon chicken prior to the game has been one of my luckier chicken dishes," Boggs told us recently. We hope it will be lucky for you too.

"Everyone I know who plays organized sports is superstitious. In baseball, players have their favorite underwear or glove, a certain meal they eat before the game, a lucky number, or a secret phrase. Superstitions may not be logical or account for what happens on the field. They're routines and rituals for the soul and spirit. They're part of your mental preparation for a game."

—*Wade Boggs, legendary slugger for the New York Yankees, in his 1990 book,* The Techniques of Modern Hitting

You'll Be Lucky . . .

. . . If you put on an article of clothing wrong side out. But you have to do this accidentally, and once you have, you must wear it that way all day.

. . . If a strange dog follows you.

. . . If you find a hairy caterpillar; throw it over your shoulder for luck.

. . . If a swallow builds a nest on your house.

. . . If a frog enters your house.

. . . If you happen to prick your finger on your birthday; let three droplets of blood fall on a clean napkin and keep the napkin.

. . . If you see three butterflies fluttering together.

"I wear my Carolina shorts every game, every day. Every single day of my life since I left college. I just feel comfortable with them on. That's where it all started for me. As long as I have these shorts on, and I have them on whether I'm playing a game or wearing a suit, I feel confident. That whole memory keeps me going . . . That was the foundation of my game, of my career."

—*Michael Jordan,* I'm Back!
More Rare Air

"If anything lucky happens to you, don't fail to go and tell it to your friends in order to annoy them."

—*Count Montroud*

The Why of Wishbones

I t's a little peculiar, when you think about it: two people grab opposite ends of a dried chicken clavicle, give it a yank, and whichever one gets the longer piece will have good luck and his or her wish will come true.

Yet almost everybody, including you, has done it—most likely more than once.

In fact, people have been yanking on wishbones ever since the third century B.C., when the Etruscans used a "hen oracle" to call upon supernatural powers to answer questions. The bird was killed, and its entrails were examined by a diviner. Then the bird's collarbone was put in the sun to dry, and the person seeking an answer from the gods made a wish on it. Afterward, two people pulled the bone apart and whoever got the larger piece got his or her wish.

In the 20th century, we tend to think of chickens as nothing more than a cheap meal, but to the ancients the cock and the hen were steeped in magical power. The hen, of course, is a prodigious layer of eggs, and almost anything associated with fertility becomes associated with luck. The cock is known for crowing at dawn, the end of night, which the ancients believed was ruled by demons. So it's natural that roosters were also associated with magic and the supernatural, and their bones were magic, too.

The bird's forked breastbone was considered especially magical because it resembles a pair of spread legs, and thus suggests fertility—the most mysterious power of all.

If you yank on that bone and get a great big piece of that power . . . well, that's the original "lucky break."

The Ladybug

The very sight of a ladybug is a good omen. If it actually lands on you, all the better! When it alights, quickly count the spots—each one represents a happy month to come. Then place it on your hand, and make a wish. When it flies off, the direction it takes is the direction from which your good luck will soon come.

At one time, the ladybug was sacred to Freya, the Norse goddess of love and beauty. Until not so long ago, young maidens in northern Europe would try to catch ladybugs, let one crawl around on the hand, and say, "She measures me for my wedding gloves."

MUCH
LUCK

SOME
LUCK

HARD
LUCK

It's Been Easy Being Green

The frog has been venerated in all places at all times—from ancient Egypt to modern Myanmar (Burma) and even in modern beer commercials. There is something about the frog that has sustained our interest through the ages.

To the ancient Egyptians the frog was a fertility symbol and an emblem of metamorphosis—for a frog's life consisted of strength growing out of weakness. It starts out as a prodigious abundance of eggs floating on water, from which tiny tadpoles emerge. Then legs and lungs develop, and they assume their final shape. Because it reproduced so prolifically, it was sacred to Heket, the goddess of childbirth.

The ancient Romans, too, were impressed by the frog's fecundity. Romans wore frog charms; the first-century scholar Pliny said a charm in the image of a frog had the power to keep love and attract friends.

Traditional American folklore, mostly by way of Europe, concentrates less on its fecundity and more on its ability to bring luck. If a frog should happen to get in your house, be thankful—good luck comes in with it. Upon seeing the first frog of spring, make a wish and it will come true. And meeting a frog on the road is good luck for the gambler.

There's an old, old myth that powdered frog's bone is a powerful medicine to subdue horses. In England some horse trainers still carry a frog's bone in their pocket.

Toads, on the other hand, are usually bad luck—although the gypsies believed a tame toad was good luck, and the Pennsylvania Dutch believed that nailing a toad's foot over the stable door kept witches out of the stable.

In the Middle Ages, people quite seriously thought that toads had a stone in their head. One medieval text advised: "If you take it when the moon is waning, put it in a linen cloth for 40 days, and then cut it from the cloth and take the stone, you will have a powerful amulet. Hung at the girdle, it cures dropsy and spleen."

Spiders

Do spiders give you the creeps? Unlikely as it may seem, they're also supposed to give you good luck.

In folklore everywhere, spiders are wise, helpful and friendly—like the spider Charlotte in the E.B. White classic *Charlotte's Web*. They are also symbols of persistence: The Scottish king Robert the Bruce was said to be inspired while in hiding by a spider who, after six failures, went on to finish its web.

But most of all, they are signals of coming prosperity. In England, small spiders are called "money-makers" or "money-spinners." If one drops down on you or in front of you, you'll be receiving a legacy or some other windfall. If it runs across your clothing, you'll be getting new clothing. Keep one in your pocket, and that pocket will never be empty of cash.

Certainly humans have learned how to catch many things by watching the spider. The lacrosse stick, for instance, was invented by Native Americans, who modeled it after the spider's web. Maybe there's a connection between a spider catching prey and you "catching" money or business. Who knows?

We do know this: Just about anywhere you go, it's bad luck to kill a spider. Hence the saying:

If you wish to live and thrive,
let the spider run alive.

The Cat Behind the Fat Cats

Every culture has good-luck charms that attract money or draw commerce to an enterprise. In Europe, spiders and spider amulets "catch" money; African-Americans use a pair of magnetic lodestones; Mexicans use magnetic horseshoes. In Japan, an ever-present statue in offices and shop windows is a cute little kitty, a *maneki-neko*. Its waving paw is supposed to lure customers.

"I think luck is the sense to recognize an opportunity and the ability to take advantage of it. Everyone has bad breaks, but everyone also has opportunities. The man who can smile at his breaks and grab his chances gets on."

—Samuel Goldwyn

"It is what a man does with his luck that makes it good or bad."

—*James A. Walker,*
Nation's Business

Ancient Recipe for a Truly Awesome Good-Luck Charm

Take a piece of polished sea-green jade, and carve upon it a perfect square. Inscribe the numbers 1, 8, 1, and 1. Set the stone in pure gold, and breathe on it three times at dawn and three times at sunset, repeating the word Thoth (an Egyptian god) five hundred times. Then tie a red thread around it.

Now no one can ever say "no" to any request you make.

Columbus's Lucky Drink

When Christopher Columbus first saw the New World on October 12, 1492, it was at least partly due to a single, extraordinarily lucky drink of water.

In the 1480s he had been but one of many adventurers who believed it would be possible to reach the spice-rich Indies by sailing west. But he'd had no luck finding a royal backer for the great voyage of discovery he proposed. Year after year he traveled through the courts of Europe, but he was repeatedly rebuffed. In all, Columbus spent eight years vainly trying to raise capital for his great "Enterprise of the Indies."

Eventually he made his

way back to the Spanish court for yet another audience with Ferdinand and Isabella. After listening to his plea, once again they turned him down. It was an insufferably hot day, so after leaving the court Columbus stopped at a nearby monastery to get a drink of water. He fell into conversation with one of the monks, and before long Columbus was pouring out his heart again, telling the holy man all about the voyage he hoped to make. The monk, it so happened, was also the Queen's confessor. And he was so taken with Columbus's speech that he spoke to Isabella, who granted Columbus yet another audience. And that time, at long last, Ferdinand and Isabella said yes.

"The highest degree of wisdom Man can possess is by no means equal to fortuitous events."

—*Joseph Addison,*
English essayist and poet

Leave Something to Chance!

On the morning before the battle of Waterloo, a young staff officer reported to the Duke of Wellington.

"All is ready, sir—nothing has been left to chance," the officer reported.

"Young man," the Duke replied, "something must always be left to chance."

Wellington went on to hand Napoleon his final defeat.

"He that leaveth
nothing to chance
will do few things
ill, but he will do
very few things."

—*George Savile, Lord Halifax,*
17th century essayist
and statesman

A Wonder Drug, Truly

If you've ever taken penicillin to get over strep throat, consider yourself lucky to be living in the last half of the twentieth century. Before World War II there was no such thing as penicillin to cure a bacterial infection. Strep throat could be fatal.

The man who gave the world penicillin was Sir Alexander Fleming, a Scottish-born bacteriologist who spent his days playing with microbes at a London teaching hospital. How he happened upon his discovery (which has been called the biggest single advance in medicine) is one of the most famous stories in modern science. Part of his work consisted of cultivating colonies of bacteria in little dishes called culture plates. One morning in September of 1928, he trotted around to his colleagues a particular culture plate on which a blob of mold had begun to grow—and was annihilating the bacteria around it.

More than a decade passed before the medical world, including Fleming himself, realized the importance of the discovery, and took it from a lab-dish specimen to a mass-produced drug. From the start, Fleming maintained that he stumbled upon penicillin by sheer accident. But it wasn't until after Fleming died in 1955 that biographers, in piecing together the historic moment, realized what astoundingly good luck it was.

In fact, "the whole chain of chance events involved in the discovery has an almost unbelievable improbability," wrote Oxford professor Gwyn Macfarlane in his 1984 biography *Alexander Fleming: The Man and the Myth.* "First, Fleming inoculates a plate with staphylococci and it happens to become contaminated with a rare, penicillin-producing strain of mould. Second, he happens not to incubate this plate. Third, he leaves it on his bench undisturbed while he is away on holiday. Fourth, the weather during this period is at first cold and then warm. Fifth, Fleming examines the plate, sees nothing interesting and discards it but, by chance, it escapes immersion in lysol. Sixth, [fellow research scholar D.M.] Pryce happens to visit Fleming's room, and Fleming decides to show him some of the many plates that had piled up on the bench. Seventh, Fleming happens to pick the discarded penicillin plate out of the tray of lysol (in which it should have been immersed), and on second inspection sees something interesting."

Other researchers had been poking around in hopes of discovering the world's first antibiotic, but Fleming was immensely lucky. As a consequence, so are we all.

"Coincidence is the language of destiny."

—*André Malraux*
French statesman and
novelist

An American in Paris

Anne Parrish was the daughter of the famous American artist Maxfield Parrish. One warm June evening, while she and her husband were browsing at a bookseller's in Paris, she came across a copy of the children's book *Jack Frost and Other Stories*. One of the most beloved books of her childhood! She excitedly passed the book to her husband, who showed the usual amount of spousal excitement for his partner's early memories—until he looked at the flyleaf. He handed back the book. There, in the handwriting of a small child, was written: "Anne Parrish, 209 N. Weber Street, Colorado Springs."

Such a lucky coincidence—how could it not change one's life? Afterward, Anne Parrish became a writer and illustrator of children's books.

"So much of life is luck. One day you make a right turn and get hit by a car. Turn left and you meet the love of your life."

—*Loretta Swit*

Old Voodoo Strategies for Luck in Love

❖ Mix up some Love Powder. Take ordinary talcum powder, color it pink or red with food coloring, and scent it with perfume. Sneak some onto your intended's body or clothing.

❖ Light a pink candle. Pink is for love and drawing people to you—unless you have to draw that person away from someone else. In that case, light a lavender candle.

"Red Fast Luck"

In a celebrated 1935 book about black folklore and culture called *Mules and Men*, writer Zora Neale Hurston included a list of ingredients for various magic rituals used by the voodoo doctors of New Orleans.

Among them is a recipe for something called "fast luck": Just add a bit of citronella oil to a bucket of wash water. When you scrub the floors of your house with this concoction, it's supposed to attract luckiness to your home—hopefully, fast. Also, Hurston adds, when you use it in a shop, "it brings luck in business by pulling customers into the store."

Another, even more potent brew, also reputed to attract luckiness, goes by the name "red fast luck." Ingredients: oil of cinnamon, oil of vanilla, and wintergreen. There's an odd magic in the making of this stuff, because though all three ingredients are gold in color, when combined they turn bright red. Mixing them up also produces a wonderfully hypnotic fragrance.

You can daub a bit on a dollar bill to attract money, daub a bit on your bedposts to attract a lover, or a daub a bit on yourself to attract luck of almost any kind.

Lucky Chain Letters

Have you ever received a chain letter in the mail? Maybe you got this one recently—it's been making the rounds. It starts off:

Kiss someone you love when you get this letter and make magic. This paper was sent to you for good luck. The original copy is in New England. It has been around the world nine times. The luck has been sent to you. You will receive good luck in four days. Send copies to people that you think need good luck. Don't send money, as fate has no price . . .

It goes on to threaten doom to anyone who breaks the chain. And there are few people, indeed, who decide to tempt fate by not sending the letter to someone they know.

These chain letters (also known as chain-of-luck letters) have circulated for generations—though they do change with the times. A famous version, the Luck of London chain letter, began circulating during Hitler's blitz of England in World War II. Another version was passed around among the soldiery of the first World War.

Because these letters appear "out of the blue," like jokes or urban myths, we were surprised to learn the origin of the very first modern chain-of-luck letter. In the early 1700s two men, Howard and Evans, had a print shop at 42 Long Lane, West Smithfield, London. They printed up a letter, which they sold for a sixpence, which they said had been written by Jesus Christ. (Uh-huh.) It read in part:

And he that hath a copy of this my own letter, written with my own hand, and spoken with my own breath, and keep-eth it, without publishing it to others, shall not prosper! But he that publisheth it to others shall be blessed of me . . . And whosoever shall have a copy of this letter, written with my hand, and keep it in their house, nothing shall hurt them . . . And goodness, happiness and prosperity, shall be in the house where a copy of this letter is to be found.

Sound familiar?

Cynical minds may scoff at the chain-of-luck letter, but there's some human wisdom at play. These letters, when passed on in multiple copies, show how quickly we can make connections with people around the world. In fact, it's all about making connections with people. And that's what luck is often all about. The more people you know, the more connections in your life, and the greater the chance that one of those connections will lead to your next lucky day.

"Geniuses are the luckiest of mortals because what they must do is the same as what they most want to do."

—*W. H. Auden*

How to Get Lucky

In a 1986 book called *How To Get Lucky*, author Max Gunther offers some useful advice about how to maximize your chances of getting a lucky break.

Life, he explains, is a sort of river of events. Lots of those events are things you planned (like getting a haircut). But some of them, as we all know, are completely unplanned, seemingly accidental occurrences (like a chance meeting with a friend), which can sometimes dramatically change your life for the better. To increase your chances of catching one of those life-changing lucky breaks, Gunther says, you need to go where the flow of events is fastest.

Whether consciously or unconsciously, lots of people who later became famous or successful have used this technique. They stay in the thick of things, circulate at parties, join clubs, keep their ears to the ground. It's people who allow themselves to become isolated and out-of-touch who are least likely to get lucky in life, Gunther says.

Why? Because lucky breaks almost always come through some other person. Luck flows along linked chains of people, even people who are "weakly linked." How many times have you heard of somebody getting a great job or meeting a terrific new person through "a friend of a friend"? Well, it's all a matter of simple mathematics. Consider these rather startling numbers.

Sociologists have estimated that the average American is in direct contact with something like 300 other people—personal "links" ranging from extremely strong (a spouse or family member) to extremely weak (the guy you see once a month at the dry cleaners). If you assume that each of those people is also weakly linked to 300 other people, that means your friend-of-a-friend network actually includes 90,000 people. And if you consider that each of those people is also in contact with 300 people, your friend-of-a-friend-of-a-friend network amounts to 27 million people!

"Networking" was one of the great buzzwords of the 1980s—and this is why it's truly important: by keeping your human connections alive, you maximize your chances of getting lucky.

Starkey's Lucky Break

Luck wasn't something that often visited Richard Starkey.

He was born July 7, 1940 in a hardscrabble working-class neighborhood in London, which he later described as "a lot of people in little boxes all trying to get out."

His mother was a barmaid, and his father worked in a bakery before he deserted the family when Richard was three.

A homely child, he was also plagued by health problems—a burst appendix at age 6 left him in a coma for ten weeks, and at 13 he developed a lung infection so severe he was taken out of school and spent the next two years in a children's sanitorium.

At 15, when Richard returned to his old school, no one remembered him. He was thin, weak and sallow and had clumps of gray hair. He could barely read or write.

He quit school and found work as a railroad messenger boy, but quit after six weeks. He got a job on a ferryboat but was fired. Eventually, through his stepfather, he became an apprentice joiner at an engineering firm.

To amuse other apprentices at lunchtime, he and another friend, Eddie, started a band. Richard became the drummer because he'd always liked to bang on things. Eventually The Eddie Clayton Skiffle Group began getting gigs at small local clubs and dance halls around London.

He joined a series of other small bands like The Raving Texans and The Hurricanes. Then one day in August, 1962, while playing at a place called Butlin's Holiday Camp, he got a telephone call from a singer he'd met in Hamburg. The singer said his band was firing its drummer and wanted Richard to take his place. (Many observers later said the main reason was that the other drummer was so good-looking that the others in the band were jealous of his ability to attract girls. Richard, with his big nose and sad-sack eyes, would offer no competition.)

By then, Richard Starkey had changed his name.

Because of his fondness for rings, he now called himself "Ringo Starr."

The name of the group was The Beatles.

And Speaking of Beetles . . .

Scarab bracelets are back in fashion, but in a sense they're timeless. The scarab has been an amulet—an object with protective power—for six thousand years.

The scarab is actually a Mediterranean beetle. It's oval in shape, like the stones of a scarab bracelet. (Long ago, the stones were carved to look just like the beetle.) Ancient Egyptians were struck by the scarab's habit of laying a single egg in a tiny ball of dung, then rolling this ball to a proper hatching place. In this mundane operation they saw a symbol for the god who rolled the sun across the sky, giving life to earth in the process. The scarab became an amulet bestowing life and fertility.

By the 4th century B.C., the Phoenicians

were mass-producing scarab amulets for sale throughout the Mediterranean and western Asia. The ancient Greeks devised a magical ceremony to perform over an emerald scarab before it was worn: they would place the scarab in an ointment of lilies, myrrh, or cinnamon for three days, then anoint themselves early in the morning with the ointment while performing a sacrifice over vine sticks.

"Charms have not their power from contracts with evil spirits, but proceed wholly from strengthening the imagination . . ."

—*Francis Bacon*

Charm Bracelets

For the girl who has everything, Tiffany & Company sells a lovely sterling-silver charm bracelet. The objects hanging off the bracelet—a toy soldier, a rocking horse, a teddy bear—are charming. They're just not charms.

The word "charm" has its roots in the Latin word *carmen*, meaning "song." Not the kind of song you'd sing in the shower, but something closer to a snake charmer's charm. Originally a charm was an incantation, a recitation of words that were supposed to possess magical power. Later the term was applied more broadly to any process, verse, word, or object that accomplished the same thing.

Another word for a charm is an amulet. The term goes all the way back to the Roman scholar Pliny, who defined the word *amuletum* as an object worn to protect the wearer against harm, bad luck, disease, the mischief of evil spirits, or the witchcraft and sorceries of one's enemies. If you want to split hairs, you could say that an amulet, according to its original meaning, is technically not a charm, but a countercharm. The charm bracelets of old were comprised of amulets that offered protection against the evil eye and other dangers of the day.

The word "talisman" means pretty much the same thing. The word probably derives from the Greek *telesm*, a consecrated statue that protected ancient cities. *Telesms* were, in effect, good-luck charms for the whole town.

By whatever name you call them, magical objects (and human trust in them) go back farther than recorded time. Archeologists who've dug up the earliest known writings—cuneiform inscriptions on clay cylinders buried under the Syrian sands—have deciphered those writings, only to discover among them a list of precious stones that could facilitate fertility and birth or induce love and hatred. In ancient Egypt, it has been noted, almost every man, woman, and child wore amulets. Charms even appear in the Bible. In Genesis 35:4, the people of Israel "gave to Jacob all the foreign gods that they had, and the ear-rings that were in their ears; and Jacob hid them under the oak which was near Sechem." In this context, it's clear that the Israelites weren't wearing ear-rings to make themselves more attractive. Their earrings were amulets.

Why "Abracadabra"?

The word "abracadabra" is an incantation, or spell, that dates back thousands of years. Some say it's derived from the old Hebrew *Ha-brachab-dabarah*, which means "speak or pronounce the Blessing"; others say it once meant "God sends forth His lightning to scatter His enemies."

Whatever it meant, it had the power to cure fevers and bring good fortune—provided it was written and recited like so:

ABRACADABRA
ABRACADABR
ABRACADAB
ABRACADA
ABRACAD
ABRACA
ABRAC
ABRA
ABR
AB
A

In the third century A.D., the Latin poet Q. Serenus wrote a medical textbook in verse in which he recommends the charm as a cure for fever. As he prescribed it: "Secretly repeat it often, but subtract the number, and more and more let each component of the form disappear, until it is reduced to a narrow cone: See to it that you wear this [written] on linen around the neck." And that's exactly what people did for 1,500 years afterward—it was widely used as late as 1665 to combat an outbreak of the plague in England that year.

As to its efficacy . . . well, it does seem to help make handkerchiefs disappear.

At Rainbow's End

If you could discover the spot where a rainbow touches earth, you'll find a pot of gold waiting for you, right? Most people know that myth from their childhood. It arrived in America with Irish immigrants, mostly, but European folklore holds that the place where the rainbow touches earth is lucky, and treasure awaits you there. In Silesia (now part of Poland) it is said that angels put the gold there, and only a naked man can carry it off! In Britain, it's lucky merely to see a rainbow, but you'll be unlucky if you point at it—a taboo that's also maintained by Native American tribes such as the Dakotas and the Hopi.

You'd be very lucky indeed if you saw a rainbow touching earth. Every rainbow is actually a circle, but the horizon cuts off your view. In other words, rainbows don't really touch the earth.

Nevertheless, a rainbow is a beautiful heavenly event; you cannot gaze at one without it touching your heart, at least. In various cultures it has been explained as a snake, a spirit, the bow of a thunder god—but most often as a bridge. Norse legend called it a soul-bridge to the land of the gods; that idea persisted in German and Austrian folk belief that the souls of children go to heaven along the rainbow, with guardian angels as their guides.

In the Bible, the rainbow is the sign of God's promise after the Flood that He will never again destroy the world with water. In that sense a rainbow is the original talisman—a supernatural object that protects us, in this case from another Deluge. Today when we see a rainbow, we're relieved to know the storm is over.

Second Time's the Charm

In Zimbabwe, people wear a good-luck charm called a *nyami-nyami*. It's cut from wood or soapstone and vaguely resembles a seahorse. The *nyami-nyami*, it's said, is the river god of the Zambezi. Legend has it that children who fall into the great river and drown are taken down into a watery underworld by the *nyami-nyami*, who gives them a second chance at life—often better than the first—since they're reborn as successful and prosperous citizens.

If Worms Don't Work

If the fish aren't biting, try chucking one of your fellow fisherfolk into the water, then haul him (or her) back out again. According to old custom, this is a good-luck charm that causes the fish to begin biting.

"A fisherman must be of contemplative mind, for it is often a long time between bites. He is by nature an optimist or he would not go fishing: for we are always going to have better luck in a few minutes or tomorrow."

—*Herbert Hoover*

Try to pick a stockbroker whose eyebrows meet in the middle—there's an old tradition that such people will be lucky in money matters all their lives.

The Mother of Invention

When he was 22, Thomas Edison closed a letter to a friend with the lines on the opposite page. At the time he was working as a low-paid telegraph operator in the Western Union office in Boston, while spending his nights trying to develop an early version of the stock-market ticker. But the invention was plagued with problems; he couldn't seem to get it to work. "No matter what I do, I reap nothing but trouble and the blues," he wrote in the same letter.

Edison's lucky ship eventually came in, of course: he went on to become one of the most prolific inventors in history, holding 1,093 patents including those for the phonograph, the incandescent light bulb— and, yes, a stock-market ticker.

"I'll never give up, for I may have a streak of luck before I die."

—*Thomas Alva Edison*

The Mark of Midas

White specks on your fingernails are said to mean good fortune, especially in money matters. There's an old saying:

> *Specks on the fingers,*
> *Money lingers*
> *Specks on the thumbs,*
> *Money comes.*

A Pocketful
of Money Charms

✤ A penny minted during a leap year is said to bring good luck in financial matters, and should always be kept as a lucky charm.

✤ It's the best of luck to come across some money you've put away and then forgotten.

✤ If you put a mark on a penny and it comes back to you, you'll inherit a fortune.

✤ It's a good idea to carry a little money in your pocket as "seed," since money attracts money.

✤ It's good luck, and an omen of prosperity, to keep the first new coin that comes into your possession after the New Year.

✤ If you find three pieces of money of the same date in your pocket, it's an omen of coming prosperity.

"If a *shlimazl* (luckless one) sold umbrellas, it would stop raining; if he sold candles, the sun would never set; and if he made coffins, people would stop dying."

—*Yiddish saying*

Something Blue

The color blue has long been associated with good luck. It goes back to the ancient idea that God lives in heaven, and since heaven is blue (at least, that's what you see when you look up there), then blue must be the color of the divine.

In some parts of the world, wearing blue beads is thought to be a potent good-luck charm because evil spirits are repelled by blue, the color of heaven.

The power of blue gave rise to an old saying: "Touch the blue and your wish will come true." And brides are advised to wear "something blue"—the blue, of course, for luck—representing respect and faith.

Lucky Wedding Customs

The many customs surrounding matrimony are part of the general happiness of the event, and they're all about good luck. Each one of them was originally a way to assure an auspicious beginning. The original meanings may have been lost over the eons, but the intention is the same as it ever was.

✤ June has been a popular month for weddings for the last 2,000 years. In Roman mythology, the goddess Juno was the devoted wife of Jupiter—and June was her month. Weddings held then were in her honor, and she blessed them.

✤ Why should a bride carry "Something old, something new, something borrowed, something blue?" The "something old" should be an article which belongs or belonged to a happily married old woman. Her good fortune would rub off on the "something new"—the bride. The "something borrowed" should be gold, which represents the sun and the source of all life. Finally, the color blue signifies respect and faithfulness—as in "true blue."

✢ Bridesmaids and groomsmen are dressed similarly to the bride and groom in order to confuse evil spirits, who could not abide to see two people so happy together. Apparently, the evil spirits of ancient Rome were easily duped.

✢ For good luck, a bride should be the first to cut her wedding cake. The groom gets his hand in as a sign that he expects to share in her good fortune. Then all the wedding guests take home a slice to have a little taste of good luck for themselves.

✢ Rice is thrown at the bride and groom as a fertility symbol to give them good luck in having children. (The Romans used to throw nuts and sweets at the bride, and the Saxons would scatter wheat and barley for her to walk upon.)

✢ An engagement ring is a diamond because its sparkle has always been believed to be the fire of love. And so long as it would sparkle, love would never cool. The diamond unites passion and constancy.

✤ A wedding ring, like the engagement ring, has been worn on the fourth finger of the left hand for millennia. It derived from the belief that there is actually a "love vein" that runs directly from the heart to that finger. A ring prevents the heart's sentiments from escaping.

✤ We say, in slang, that two people "tied the knot." Once upon a time, a bride and groom really did tie a knot in a cord or ribbon as part of the ceremony. Or she would arrive at the altar with an untied shoe, and he would tie the lace as part of the ceremony. Knots were also tied in the bride's bouquet as a way to keep the day's good wishes from escaping.

✤ The term "honeymoon" derives from the Teutonic custom in which the bride and groom drank mead for one month or "moon" (a lunar cycle is 28 days) after the wedding.

✤ The bride is carried over the threshold to her new home in order to keep her from tripping—a terrible omen. Why would she trip? Because of those evil spirits, of course: they might be lurking at the doorway, hoping to trip her up.

Sing Hallelujah!

The choir practice was scheduled for 7:20 P.M. Well, 7:20 came and went, and not one of the 15 choir members had shown up. Not the minister and his family—his wife was still ironing her dress. Another mother and daughter were delayed because the mother couldn't rouse the daughter from a nap. One girl was delayed by geometry homework; another couldn't start her car . . . All in all, 10 ordinary excuses kept the 15-member choir from arriving on time.

Lucky them. At 7:25 on the evening of March 1, 1950, the little church in Beatrice, Nebraska, was destroyed by an explosion.

Choir members wondered whether their tardiness was an act of God. It sure wasn't the force of probability: the odds against everyone being late on the same night was less than one in a million.

When good luck comes to you, invite her in.

—*Spanish proverb*

Good-Luck Charm of the Gods

Of all the stones that have become associated with good luck, probably none has as illustrious a history as jade.

In New Zealand, the Maori people wear charms made of local jade or greenstone because they're said to bring good fortune to the wearer. A highly prized jade charm, called a *hei-tiki*, is often buried with its owner.

In China, babies used to be fitted with jade bracelets; if the bracelet never broke, it was said to portend great good luck for the child for the rest of its life.

In India, jade was considered so sacred and powerful that in ancient times no one except royalty was even allowed to own it on pain of death.

There's an old Chinese legend about a

youth chasing a butterfly who entered the garden of a rich mandarin and instead of being thrown out, wound up marrying the mandarin's daughter. That's why jade butterflies have become a symbol of luck in love; Chinese bridegrooms will sometimes present jade butterflies to their fiancées.

But it's not just long ago and far away that jade has been valued: jazz great Lionel Hampton wore an enormous jade ring to his concerts for good luck.

China, of course, is the place you think of as having the greatest reverence for jade—in fact, since ancient times it's been looked on there as "an almost divine material," writes Frank Davis in a little book called *Chinese Jade*. But the amazing fact is that jade has been treasured as a talisman and lucky charm in cultures around the world—by the Greeks, Romans, Aztecs, Mayans, and even the Eskimos, who consider it a good-luck charm for fishing.

There's also a very ancient tradition, dating back to Egyptian times and mentioned by Galen in the first century A.D., that jade and green jaspers have great healing powers, especially for diseases of the kidneys and urinary tract. When the Spaniards were pillaging South America, they found many ornaments and amulets made of jade or jadeite, which the natives used as charms against kidney stones. That's where the name "jade" came from in the first place: it's a shortened form of the Spanish *piedra de hijada*, meaning "stone of the flank."

It's not hard to understand all this adoration of jade: It's extraordinarily beautiful, especially when polished, and can range in color from translucent green to pure white, yellow, orange, or black. (Usually the greenest stone is considered the most valuable and the luckiest.) It's quite rare, and always has been. (Those little figurines that are exported from Hong Kong by the boatload are only rarely jade; usually they're softer, cheaper stones like alabaster or fluorite.) And it's extremely hard—so hard that it's almost impossible to scratch, even with a metal tool.

There's one other little thing about jade that's magical, Davis writes: It's "always cool to the touch, and this is one of many qualities which caused jade to be so highly valued among the Chinese, who were in the habit of carrying a piece about with them, no doubt partly as a luck-bringer but also because it is so pleasant to handle."

Buckeye Luck

Horse chestnuts, or "buckeyes," are brown satin-shiny nuts, flat on one side and about the size of an overgrown acorn, that feel wonderful in your hand. (They're popularly known as buckeyes because the nut has a pale, circular scar on the flat side that vaguely resembles the eye of a deer.)

In many different countries all over the world, horse chestnuts are carried to bring good luck and also good health. In the American South, people carry them around in their pockets to prevent rheumatism or (if you've already got it) to lessen its pain. Elsewhere, buckeyes are thought to prevent headaches. And sometimes tea made from horse-chestnut blossoms is drunk to cure a host of other ills.

It's hard to know exactly how the buckeye got linked to luck. Some have suggested it's because of the "doctrine of signatures," the ancient, magical notion that "like brings like." Since the buckeye tree is unusually long-lived, it may have become associated with long life and hence with good health and luck. Others have pointed out that a buckeye rather resembles a human testicle, and hence might suggest fertility or sexual prowess—luck in love. (Almost anything associated with love or fertility has been considered lucky at one time or another.)

But our favorite explanation is the simplest: If you walk underneath a buckeye tree and see a scatter of shiny nuts, it's almost impossible not to stop and pick one up. And when you do, you'll notice how irresistibly smooth and pleasant it feels in your palm. Stroking it with a thumb or finger just feels good. It's comforting, somehow, in the way that a teddy bear is comforting to a child.

Feeling comforted, feeling safe, feeling satisfied. That is a little like feeling lucky.

Salt Luck

All kinds of luck lore is associated with salt, something so cheap and so plentiful we barely think about it today. In ancient times, though, salt was both hard to come by and highly valued—so highly valued, in fact, that a few telling phrases have survived to this day. When a man isn't valued very much, we still say he's "not worth his salt." If you don't believe something, you "take it with a grain of salt." And in ancient times, workers were paid with salt. That's where we get our word "salary."

Because it preserved meat and other foods from decay, the discovery of salt was a monumental event in human history. And it's not terribly surprising that it quickly took on magical properties. Salt became associated with anything that doesn't decay, that's unchanging, immutable, immortal. It became part of many sacred rituals, especially those having to do with making an oath or pledge (an agreement that's supposed to be unbroken or unchanging). "Taking salt together" was said to bind two people in eternal friendship. "There is salt between us" is an old expression that means "we're friends."

Salt was also associated with the idea of keeping evil spirits (bad luck) at bay. That's why, if you spill salt, you're supposed to throw a pinch over your left shoulder. Not only is the left side often associated with unluckiness or evil ("sinister" is the Latin word for left), but there's nothing evil spirits hate more than getting salt in their eyes!

New House Luck

✤ To bring luck to a new house, go into every room holding a loaf of bread and a dish of salt. This old custom is sometimes known in the western part of England as "house-handsel." "Handsel" comes from an Old English word, *handselen*, "hand gift," a gift put into the hand that brings good luck.

✤ "Housewarming" presents were originally meant to bring good luck to a new household. They still can, you know.

✤ It is lucky to move to a new house on a Monday or a Wednesday. Friday is an unlucky moving day. (The Pennsylvania Dutch have a saying: "Friday flitting; short sitting." You won't be living there long, in other words.)

✤ Never move downstairs in the same building.

✤ If you can, send a new broom in advance of your move. That's good luck. But never move a broom from one house to another.

Getting Off on the Right Foot

There's a very old idea that the right side of anything is associated with good luck, and the left side, with bad.

The Romans feared that someone who entered a place with the left foot first would bring in bad luck. In public places guards were stationed at the entrance to make sure every visitor got off on the right foot. And noble families employed "footmen" for the same reason. A person who stands by the door of a fancy hotel is still called a footman because of this ancient luck custom.

According to an ancient tradition, if your right ear or right eye tingles, it's a lucky omen, meaning that a friend is speaking about you.

If your right palm itches, it means that money's coming.

The Old Man at the Fort

An old man was living with his son at an abandoned fort on top of a hill, and one day he lost a horse. The neighbors came to express their sympathy for this misfortune, and the old man asked, "How do you know this is bad luck?" A few days later his horse returned with a number of wild horses. His neighbors came again to congratulate him on this stroke of fortune, and the old man replied, "How do you know this is good luck?" With so many horses around, his son took to riding, and one day he broke his leg. Again the neighbors came around to express their sympathy, and the old man replied, "How do you know this is bad luck?" The next year there was a war, and because the old man's son was crippled, he did not have to go to the front.

—Taoist parable

Common Antidotes for Bad Luck

✤ If you get up on the left (wrong) side of the bed, put your right sock and shoe on first.

✤ If you spill salt, throw some over your left shoulder. It will hit the Devil in the face.

✤ If you pass someone on the stairs, cross your fingers.

✤ If you break a mirror, wash the broken pieces in a south-running river.

✤ If you're walking with others in a row, and a passerby or tree or any large object separates you, say "bread and butter" and cross your fingers. Or make a cross on the sidewalk with your foot.

✤ If you stumble, especially at the entrance to a home or upon embarking on a trip, go back and pass once more without tripping.

"Behind bad luck comes good luck."

—*Gypsy proverb*

Good Luck
Disguised as Bad

In September 1795, a 21-year-old army officer named Meriwether Lewis was serving under General Wayne in what was then the western frontier but is now Ohio. One day, when seriously intoxicated, Lewis burst into the home of another officer, a Lieutenant Elliot, and became embroiled in a ferocious argument about politics. Elliot threw Lewis out of his house. Still angry, drunk, and agitated, Lewis returned later the same day and challenged Elliot to a duel.

The duel never occurred—but several weeks later, Elliot had Lewis hauled in front of a general court-martial for his behavior. Lewis pleaded not guilty to the charges. Testimony was taken; the trial lasted almost a week. In the end, the officers of the court agreed with Lewis's version of events, and he was acquitted.

Nevertheless, General Wayne felt it was wisest that the two young officers be separated, so he had Lewis transferred to a different regiment—the Chosen Rifle Company of elite riflemen-sharpshooters. The captain of that company was a man named William Clark. So it was that a famous partnership in American history, Lewis and Clark, resulted from a low-down drunken squabble.

Sometimes things happen that appear to be bad luck, perhaps even disastrously bad luck, but later turn out to have been good luck after all. . . .

JFK's Lucky Loss

In 1956, when the Democratic Party was looking for a vice-presidential nominee to run on the ticket with Adlai Stevenson, one of the most promising candidates was a dashing young senator from Massachusetts named John F. Kennedy. Kennedy was widely favored to win the nomination. But in a stunning, last-minute upset, the party chose Senator Estes Kefauver of Tennessee instead. Kennedy was bitterly disappointed.

That night, sitting in a hotel room, JFK's younger brother Bobby tried to console him. "You're better off than you ever were in your life, and you made a great fight, and they're not going to win, and you're going to be the candidate next time," Bobby was quoted as telling Jack.

Sounds like one of those lame cheering-up speeches—but Bobby turned out to be

right. Stevenson and Kefauver were defeated
by Eisenhower and Nixon in a landslide. And
many historians now believe that, had
Kennedy been on the Stevenson ticket,
they'd still have lost, which would have done
great political damage to Kennedy. So much
damage that he probably would not have
been nominated for president four years
later in 1960.

Sing It Again, Bea

Some years ago the Noel Coward revue *This Year of Grace*, was touring Canada after a season on Broadway. Playing the leading role was famed British actress Beatrice Lillie. During their stint in London, Ontario, they were performing one afternoon, and the show had gotten around to Miss Lillie's song "Brittania Rules the Waves." During the second verse of the song, the show's "blocking" called for the cast to move to center stage for the chorus.

But during this particular matinée, Miss Lillie made a most uncharacteristic mistake. She repeated the second verse! And so the members of cast stayed glued to their spots, awaiting their cue to move. Suddenly a huge arc light fell and crashed in center stage—precisely where the cast would have been if Miss Lillie had not repeated herself.

Thanks—I Needed That

When director George Miller was looking for someone to play the male lead for his 1979 post-Apocalypse road movie *Mad Max*, he was specifically looking for someone who looked weary, beaten-up, and scarred.

One of the many "wannabes" who answered the cattle call for the part was a then-unknown Australian actor named Mel Gibson. It just so happened that the night before his scheduled screen test, Gibson was attacked, and badly beaten up, by three drunks. When he showed up for the audition the next morning looking like a prize fighter on a losing streak, Miller gave him the part. It launched Gibson's career as an international movie star in such films as *The Year of Living Dangerously*, *Lethal Weapon*, and the 1995 Oscar-winning *Braveheart*.

The Billion-Dollar Break

Omaha billionaire Warren Buffett is the second richest man in America. He's built his fortune over a lifetime of shrewd investments. But he didn't always have it easy. At age 20 he was rejected by Harvard Business School.

The day he got the rejection letter he went to a library and began researching other business schools. And it wasn't until then that he noticed that Benjamin Graham and David Dodd, whose book *Security Analysis* he so admired, both taught at Columbia. He applied at the last minute—and was accepted. There he got to know Graham, who was to become his mentor and boss.

Buffett once told *Fortune* that when he looks back on it now, he concludes: "Probably the luckiest thing that ever happened to me was getting rejected from Harvard."

"Luck is a mighty queer thing. All you know about it for certain is that it's bound to change."

—*Bret Harte,*
American writer

Believe It or Not!

Getting shot is almost certainly bad luck. But every once in a while, some miraculous turn of good luck intervenes to save a life. As in these cases, recorded in the 100th Anniversary edition of *Ripley's Believe It Or Not!*:

✦ Oliver Anthony, of Memphis, Tennessee, was shot by a robber while playing golf one day. He survived only because the bullet hit a golf ball in his pocket—and lodged there.

✦ Detective Melvin G. Lobbett, of Buffalo, New York, was shot by a .38-caliber bullet at close range. But he survived because the bullet hit his badge—which he'd dropped into his coat pocket only a moment before the shooting.

✦ Angel Santana of New York City escaped injury when a robber's bullet bounced off his pants zipper. (Angel's guardian angel must have a strange sense of humor!)

"Fortuna is constant only in her inconstancy."

—Ovid

The Luckiest Guy in History

Muzafar Jang, an eighteenth-century rebel leader in Deccan, India, was sentenced to be executed. He was tied to the mouth of a cannon, and was about to be blown to bits—when suddenly a messenger rode up. The ruler who'd ordered his execution had died, and the elected successor was none other than . . . Muzafar Jang! One minute he's about to die a horrible death; the next minute he's the ruler of 35 million people.

Are You Ready for Luck?

"If bad luck can wrench control from our grasp, so can good luck. The bold are ready to grab a piece of good luck when it drifts by, even if it means going off in a new, unplanned direction. They don't try to control their lives so rigidly that they ignore lucky breaks lying off the main track . . .

"If something goes right, don't argue. Or, to put it another way: When good luck pulls you sideways, let go."

—*Max Gunther,* The Luck Factor

The Lucky Elephant

Why are images or carvings of elephants so widely cherished as good-luck charms? Is it because of the elephant's famous memory, intelligence, strength, or longevity? Perhaps. Among the Hindus, the elephant-headed god Ganesha is said to bring luck to new enterprises because he's the remover of obstacles. In India, Ganesha's lucky image is often seen at the entrance to temples or houses.

White Animals

When news got out that a white buffalo calf named Miracle had been born on a farm in Janesville, Wisconsin in 1994, Native Americans converged from all across the country. Some of them drove thousands of miles to see the little animal, bringing gifts of sweet grass, alabaster, and eagle feathers, because to native peoples, the white buffalo is a stirring symbol of hope, rebirth, and unity among the tribes.

But Native Americans aren't the only ones to revere white animals. In many cultures from around the world, mystic power—and luckiness—is associated with white hens, rabbits, elephants, horses, owls, and butterflies. In Roman times, somebody who was extraordinarily lucky was referred to as a "son of a white hen." White rabbits (except for the one who led Alice down the rabbit hole) have long been considered a sign of good luck in England.

When he was invading Ireland in 1171, the British king Henry II saw a white hare jump out of a nearby hedge. The king's soldiers immediately captured the animal and presented it to him as a good-luck charm.

Owning a white horse is said to be good luck and to ensure a long life. If you see a white horse, it's a lucky sign and an omen that you'll soon find something good. To make sure the luck works, recite this little charm:

> *White, white, white horse,*
> *Sing, sing, sing,*
> *On my way I'll find something.*

A white elephant has come to mean some useless, often ridiculous object, like a sofa made out of a pink Cadillac. But in many places in Asia, white elephants have always been greatly revered. In ancient times the monarch of Burma was called "the king of the white elephants." The white elephant was considered sacred and a bringer of good luck.

By old custom, it's bad luck to kill a white deer.

In India, the white owl is sacred to the goddess of prosperity—it's very lucky when one builds its nest in your house.

If the first butterfly you see in the new year is white, that's very good luck indeed.

And if you see a white cricket, it means an absent lover will return.

Grass-Larks for Luck

There's a very old tradition, ranging from China and India to the British Isles, that a cricket chirping in the house means good luck—and that killing a cricket (like killing a ladybug or a spider) will bring bad luck. In Japan, where there are at least a dozen different kinds of crickets with wonderful names like "grass-lark" or "bell-insect," people have kept them inside their houses in tiny bamboo cages as a kind of living good-luck charm since at least the tenth century.

In olden times crickets often crept into houses in bad weather, setting up shop someplace where it was warm (such as near the hearth). Besides providing free music, a cricket on the hearth was valued because it became the housewife's barometer, fore-telling rain (since crickets often chirp louder before rain). Eventually crickets came to be associated with mirth, prosperity, hospitality, and luck.

In rural England, crickets were referred to as "gentle wee things," the word "gentle" being a code word for fairy birth. To kill a cricket—a fairy, in other words—was very bad luck indeed. Among the Irish, there's a superstition that crickets are enchanted beings, hundreds of years old; and that if we could understand what they're saying, they'd tell us the history of the world.

No wonder it's good luck to have them around!

How to Change
Bad Luck to Good

Pull a pocket inside out.

Walk up a flight of stairs backwards.

Turn around three times. This is in accordance with the old rhyme, "I turn myself three times about, and thus I put bad luck to rout."

Three's the Charm

"Third time's the charm," people sometimes say, usually after flubbing their first two tries at something.

Maybe they don't realize that the number three has been considered the luckiest of all numbers for thousands of years in cultures and religions all over the world—a number that's supposed to have supernatural power and work as a charm.

Though the numbers seven and nine are also thought to have deep mystic significance, "of all the numbers in the infinite scale none has been more universally revered than three," writes Philip Waterman in *The Story of Superstition*.

That's probably why so many lucky rituals are supposed to be repeated three times. For instance, in order to reverse his luck, a gambler on a losing streak is supposed to get

up and walk around his chair three times. Or
why so many folk medicines involve three
ingredients. Or why, in China, the third day
of a new moon is said to be the most fortunate day of the month.

As long ago as the 6th century B.C., the
Greek philosopher Pythagoras had concluded that three was "the perfect number."
And the triangle, with its three sides—the
most stable of all forms—was considered a
magic symbol. In many cultures, it was supposed to have the power to repel the Devil.
That's why it's supposed to be bad luck to
walk underneath a leaning ladder: because
you break the sacred triangle.

For Christians, of course, three signifies
the Trinity. In folk tradition, no good-luck
charm will work unless you say afterwards,
"in the name of the Father, the Son and Holy
Ghost."

Some scholars say three originally took
on sacred significance because the moon,

linked to so many superstitions, has three phases—full, waxing, and waning. Of course, there's also the fact that almost everything has a beginning, a middle, and an end. An ideal family includes man, woman, and child. A human being has body, soul, and spirit. There's past, present, and future. Animal, vegetable, mineral. Three wishes. Three cheers. Three strikes.

Good luck.

Good luck.

Good luck!

Sneezing has been considered a strong omen of good luck since ancient times. It's especially good luck if you sneeze three times in a row.

The Table of Jupiter

Until as recently as the seventeenth century, people wore "magic squares" around the neck. These were a series of magic numbers, printed on paper or metal, that provided protection. One such charm was the Table of Jupiter. The following numbers were etched on a thin plate of silver, made when Jupiter is ascendant:

4	14	15	1
9	7	6	12
5	11	10	8
16	2	3	13

Notice that whichever way you add the columns—horizontally or vertically—the total is the same: 34. And in numerology, 34 means 7 because the 3 and 4 are added together. The number 7 has been lucky for a long, long time. . . .

It's good luck to have seven letters in either your first or your last name.

Lucky Seven

The notion that seven is a lucky number comes from the dice game of "craps." If you roll a seven on the first try, you win. Also noteworthy is this fact: Pick up any die (that's the singular of dice) and add together any two opposite sides. The number you'll always come up with? Seven.

If "craps" seems old-fashioned in this modern age of gambling, well, it is. It's several centuries old. Even so, it's not as old as dice—they're a few thousand years old. But

human fascination with the number seven is even older than that. It's always been a number of completion; important things have to be seven in number to be somehow fitting. There are seven seas, seven graces, seven heavens, seven deadly sins, seven days of the week, seven wonders of the world. And, yes, even seven dwarfs.

To the ancient Greeks, seven was a perfect number. It's the sum of three and four, the triangle and the square, which were regarded as the two perfect figures. Much of Jewish ritual was governed by this number. The Arabs had seven holy temples; the Hindus supposed the world to be enclosed within the compass of seven peninsulas; Norse mythology had seven deities; in the Persian mysteries were seven caverns through which the seeker of truth had to pass. And most ancient sacrifices were never complete unless seven victims were sent to their deaths.

All this has been traced back to that primeval regulator of time on earth: the moon and its phases. The lunar cycle is 28 days (seven times four), and every seven days the moon begins a new phase. If there's any mystery as to why seven is a lucky number, it was solved in 1913, in one sentence from *An Encyclopedia of Freemasonry:* "In the Hebrew, Syrian, Persian, Phoenician, Chaldean, and Saxon, the word Seven signifies full or complete, and every seventh day after the first quarter the moon is complete in its change."

Lucky 13?

The number 13 is so widely associated with bad luck that most tall buildings don't have a thirteenth floor, most hotels lack a room number 13, and 13 loaves of bread are called a "baker's dozen" rather than the name of that dreaded number.

There's even a word for the fear of 13: "triskaidekaphobia."

But it hasn't always been that way.

There's an old folk tradition that any child born on the thirteenth of the month will be lucky in everything he (or she) does.

The Aztecs thought 13 had a mystic significance, and built 13 steps up to the sacred platforms where they kept sacred fires burning. The Mayans worshipped "the 13 gods of the upper world." Even modern Judaism accords the number 13 a special significance.

Every Orthodox Jewish prayerbook contains "The Thirteen Principles of Faith" and extolls the 13 attributes of God. Jewish boys celebrate their Bar Mitzvah at age 13.

Thirteen has always been an especially fortunate number for Americans. After all, the United States grew out of 13 colonies, which is why the U.S. flag still bears 13 stripes. And take a look at the Great Seal Of The United States on the back of a dollar bill. It depicts an eagle with 13 stars above its head, a shield bearing 13 stripes, and a motto ("E Pluribus Unum") with 13 letters. The bird is holding in one claw 13 arrows and in the other a laurel branch with 13 leaves—and if you look closely, 13 olives.

Lodes of Luck

The basic idea behind all lucky charms is that in some magical way they'll attract luck—almost the same way that a magnet attracts iron. So it should come as no surprise that since ancient times, magnets have been used as good-luck charms.

Actually, we're not talking about man-made metal magnets here; we're talking about magnetic iron ore, a naturally occurring, lustrous black stone that's sometimes called magnetite or lodestone. Pliny the Elder, the first-century Roman naturalist, reports that a Greek shepherd named Magnes first discovered the magic rocks when one of them clung to the nails on his shoe when he was tending sheep. That happy accident made the lowly shepherd famous, since we still remember him every time we use the word "magnetism."

By 800 B.C., these amazing stones were
being eagerly mined in Thessaly, and people
had come to believe that they could not only
attract iron but all sorts of other good things.
In the East Indies, for instance, they were
thought to attract power, favor, and good fortune—which is why upwardly mobile kings
were always crowned in thrones made of
lodestone. And Alexander the Great gave all
his soldiers lodestones, believing they were
powerful good-luck charms, as well as a
sure-fire defense against enchantments and
evil spirits.

Another magical idea that became
associated with lodestones was that they
could help people get lucky in love. It's not
hard to understand why: In languages as
dissimilar as Chinese and Sanskrit, there's
the notion that the way lodestone attracts
iron is similar to the way two lovers are
attracted to each other. In Sanskrit the
word for lodestone is *chumbaka*, or "the

kisser"; in Chinese, it's *t'su shi*, or "the
loving-stone."

From there it's only a short leap to the
old Spanish belief that if a lover wishes the
love of a lady, no matter how cold she may
be, all he has to do is grind up a little bit of
lodestone, swallow it before bed, and she'll
be magnetically attracted to him.

In a strange medieval remedy book
called the *Poor-man's Treasury*, there's this
solemn advice: to help soothe strife and dis-

cord between a man and a woman, try wearing a lodestone around your neck.

And then there's the bizarre trial that
took place in July 1887 in the American

South. A woman sued a conjurer to recover five dollars she'd paid him for a piece of lodestone, which she intended to use as a sort of love magnet to bring back her wandering husband. Since the going rate for lodestone was 75 cents a pound, and this piece only weighed a few ounces, the judge ordered that the woman get her money back. No telling what happened to the husband.

One ancient writer waxes positively rhapsodic about the virtues of the lodestone: "With this stone, you can hear the voices of the gods and learn many wonderful things . . . It is a glorious remedy against wounds, bites of snakes, headache, and it will make the deaf hear."

With a lucky charm like that, how can you go wrong?

"Fortune may have yet a better success in reserve for you, and they who lose today may win tomorrow."

—*Miguel de Cervantes,* Don Quixote

Why the Horseshoe
Is Lucky

Chances are, within walking distance of where you are at this very moment, there's a horseshoe nailed up over somebody's door for luck. (It's probably attached with the points facing upward so the luck "won't spill out.") You'd be as likely to find one if you were in Tokyo, Cairo, or Dubuque, Iowa—because belief in the luck-attracting power of the horseshoe is nearly universal.

Like most other lucky objects, it's best if you find the horseshoe, or are given it as a gift, rather than buying it yourself. Another tradition holds that you shouldn't pull out any of the nails; you'll keep your luck as many years as there are nails.

Why is the horseshoe such a potent charm? Perhaps because it combines three different things that have been associated with good luck since ancient times: the horse, iron, and the crescent shape.

Horses have long been worshipped as magical animals, and any part of them may be linked to luck or good fortune. (China is one of the few places where horseshoes aren't considered lucky—but horse's hooves are.)

Iron has been associated with magical power since ancient times, and it's not hard to understand why. Our first contact with it was in the form of meteors—fiery missiles that came hurtling down from heaven, perhaps from God. And when people learned to fashion weapons from these odd, crumpled hunks of metal, they discovered it to be extraordinarily effective in hunting and in battle. Shields and armor fashioned of iron made a warrior practically invulnerable to attack. Who would not conclude that there must be some protective magic, perhaps divine, associated with iron? From Scotland to

Morocco, traditional belief is that iron is a charm against ghosts, witches, demons, and all dangerous spirits.

So horseshoes—or anything else made of iron—came to be seen as a protection. In the first century A.D., the Roman author Pliny wrote that people would remove iron nails from coffins and lay them on the lintel above their bedroom doors to keep away the Devil. And even today, in rural Ireland, country folk believe that no harm or ill luck ever comes to a blacksmith.

But perhaps the most potent aspect of a horseshoe is its crescent shape. Horseshoes resemble the horned new moon, which is an old, old symbol for the female life-creating force. It was the symbol of the Egyptian goddess Isis, the Greek goddess Artemis, the Roman goddess Diana, the Babylonian goddess Ishtar—Great Mother figures, all. Nailing a horseshoe over the door, in effect, is a way of fighting the forces of death with the forces of life. In ancient Yucatán and Peru there were temples with arched doorways, with engravings of the female creator above them.

America got its horseshoe traditions by way of Britain, mostly. "That the horseshoe may never be pulled from your threshold!" was a common English way of wishing someone well. Britain's famous naval hero, Lord Nelson, had a horseshoe nailed to the mast of his ship, *Victory*. And the ancient Druids seemed to see some mystic significance in the horseshoe shape: that's what Stonehenge looks like from the air.

"Popularity and glamour are only part of the factors involved in winning elections. One of the most important of all is luck. In my own case, luck was always with me . . ."

—*Harry Truman*, Memoirs

The Luckiest President

He wasn't a lawyer, never went to college, and he wasn't born rich. He tried to make a go of business, but all his efforts—a clothing store, an oil-drilling partnership, a zinc mine—met with failure.

Luckily, he ended up as President.

Harry Truman was a lonely, serious child and a self-admitted sissy. Because of his poor eyesight, he was turned down by West Point. But he was a good student, and would have gone off to college somewhere—except for his father's bad luck. Just as he was graduating from high school, his father lost nearly everything by gambling on wheat futures. Within a few years, Harry would be plowing his grandfather's farm.

World War I gave him a chance to escape that life, and after coming home he started a men's clothing store in Kansas City. That failed in 1922, when falling farm prices threw the American heartland into a recession. He was 38 years old, and between him and his partner, he was $35,000 in debt. Rather than declare bankruptcy, he would spend the next 15 years paying off the loans. He would be strapped for cash until he was nearly 60.

But just as his haberdashery was going under, Truman's luck changed. One of his Army pals was the heir apparent to Kansas City's Pendergast machine, and the Pendergasts put him up for county judge (an administrative post). He won. When he was 42, he ran for presiding judge and won. Perhaps all his bad luck had really been good luck—because he'd finally found his calling.

On the day he turned 50, he saw nothing more for himself than virtual retirement in some minor county office. A week later, the Pendergast machine asked him to run for the U.S. Senate. Luckily for Truman, the Pendergasts had been turned down by three other potential candidates. In the Democratic primary he was up against two better-known Missouri congressmen who coveted the seat. But he beat them, and went on to win in the general election.

Six years later, in 1940, he had to run for reelection against a popular governor. He was shunned, personally and politically, by President Roosevelt. He had so little money that, when he was out on the campaign trail, he slept in his car. Luckily, Missouri's other senator, Champ Clark, threw his weight behind Truman at the last minute and delivered the vote in St. Louis.

In 1944 the Democratic convention dumped then vice-president Henry Wallace, and nominated Truman as the running mate for an ailing FDR. They won. And FDR would live all of 82 days into his fourth term.

So Truman was sworn in—but this unremarkable man with the flat Missouri accent was universally regarded as an accidental president, and the least likely of men to succeed so dashing a figure as FDR. By 1948, when it came time to run for president on his own, he was being written off again. The press and the polls said he was finished. Everyone assumed Thomas E. Dewey would be the next president.

Truman pulled off the biggest political upset in American presidential history.

Luck was with him once again in 1950, when he survived an assassination attempt by two Puerto Rican nationalists. Right after the incident, he told his naval aide, Admiral William Leahy, that the only thing to worry about was bad luck, and that was something he never had.

Maybe it was the horseshoe ashtray he kept on his Oval Office desk. Or the horseshoe his father hung over the door of the house in Lamar, Missouri, the day Harry was born.

Lucky Losers

Some people are so lucky that, when they lose something, it's not really lost. Consider:

✤ The man who lost his fountain pen in South Carolina; his wife found it three years later on the street in New York . . .

✤ The Maine lobsterman whose glasses fell overboard, and were found in his brother's lobster trap . . .

✤ The man who lost his worker-identification badge while fishing in Long Island Sound, and hooked it in the same spot two months later . . .

✤ The German farmer's wife who lost her wedding ring in a potato field. Forty years later she found it— inside a potato from that field.

What a Find!

This story will fire the imagination of anyone who has ever pulled over to the curb to scout out a garage sale.

In the "Amish country" of Lancaster County, Pennsylvania, there's a strip of flea markets and antiques dealers just south of Adamstown on Route 272. One day in 1989, a lucky fellow was browsing among the stalls when he spotted a torn painting of a dismal country scene. Well, at least the price was right: four bucks. He handed over the $4 only because he wanted the gilded frame.

When he got home, he removed the torn painting—and found something tucked behind it. He carefully unfolded it, only to find himself staring at a crisp, clean copy of the Declaration of Independence.

As it turns out, the copy was printed on

July 4, 1776, by John Dunlap of Philadelphia, to carry the day's big news to the citizens of the 13 colonies. It's one of only 25 known copies of the Declaration, and one of only three remaining in private hands.

In June 1991, the man (who remained anonymous) sold his lucky find at Sotheby's, the famous New York auction house. The price that day: $2.4 million.

More Lucky Finds

Sotheby's is the auction house in New York where the world's finest art, antiques, and collectibles come up for sale. The experts on staff there are always hearing stories of incredible good luck. The tellers are often ordinary people who happen to come upon objects, not knowing their worth—and they end up at Sotheby's because the items are so rare and valuable. Among the examples of recent years . . .

One winter's day in 1988 a fisherman was looking among old farming pamphlets at a roadside antiques barn in southern New Hampshire. He picked up a book priced at $18 and offered $15. The book turned out to be an 1827 first edition of *Tamerlane*, the poems of Edgar Allen Poe. The volume is known as "the black tulip" among book collectors because it is the rarest book in American literature—only a dozen copies survive. The man later sold it at auction for $198,000.

A Connecticut woman was at her grandparents' house one day when they were throwing out paintings. She saved one for herself. It hung over her bed for 25 years. Finally she took it to a local art dealer, who offered her $1,000. Later that day, the dealer called her back and offered her $100,000. Eventually the painting was sold at a 1989 auction for $1.1 million. It was a rare work by the nineteenth-century American artist Martin Johnson Heade.

A British couple bought a garden statue for about $10 back in the 1950s, and it decorated their garden for three decades. When they decided to sell it, it turned out to be a previously undiscovered work of the Renaissance master Adrien de Vries. It sold at a 1989 auction for $10.7 million. Now it's dancing at the Getty Museum in Malibu, California.

Button Bracelets

Buttons that are given to you as a gift are good luck. (By tradition, most good luck charms work only if they're given or received as gifts.) Sometimes people will make good-luck bracelets out of buttons they've received as gifts. As long as the button bracelet is worn, so the legend goes, the friendship cannot be broken.

Finders Keepers

To find any of the following things is very good luck.

✦ Anything purple

✦ Yellow ribbon, especially if it's floating on water (this presages gold)

✦ A postage stamp

✦ A pencil

✦ A Native American arrowhead

✦ A four-leaf clover

✦ A clean napkin

✦ A horseshoe

✦ A pin. Hence the old ditty: "See a pin and pick it up/All the day you'll have good luck."

✦ A button. You'll get as many unexpected dollars as there are holes in the button.

✦ A coin. You should never pass up a coin, even a penny, because if you do, your luck will pass to the person who picks it up.

It's especially good luck to find a penny head side up.

The Lucky Penny

At every convenience store there's a little dish beside the cash register, so you can "give a penny, take a penny" as you wish.

This harks back to the ancient custom of exchanging "luck money" after a purchase. In rural areas of Europe, someone who sold a horse or a cow always remembered to return some small part of the purchase price to the buyer—even a penny would do. This "luck money," it was believed, ensured that the animal would stay healthy and the business deal would not go sour.

Maybe it's magic. But it's also a bit of wisdom distilled from centuries of human experience: an act of generosity can bring back far more than you give away.

Keep a leap-year penny in the kitchen to bring un-expected windfalls your way.

Three Coins in the Fountain

Who can resist throwing coins into a well or a fountain for luck or to make a wish come true? But almost nobody re-members where this old custom comes from: the ancient belief that spirits dwell at the bottom of springs and fountains, and they demand tribute.

In some ancient societies this belief was taken so seriously that people were willing to pay the ultimate price, sacrificing one of their own flesh and blood to appease the fountain gods and thus ensure the prosperity of the entire town. In the Well of Sacrifice in Chichen Itza, Mexico, young Mayan girls were thrown to their deaths for good luck. According to legend, at least, the girls didn't mind the inconvenience—they believed that the spirits of the well, impressed by such self-sacrifice, would marry them and they'd live happily ever after in some never-never land beneath the water.

Nowadays, most of us are content to toss a small coin into the fountain for luck.

"Imagine, if you can, a luck-less world, where everything could be planned and nothing unexpected ever happened. Such a world would be the dullest place that could possibly be conceived."

—*Lothrop Stoddard,* Luck: Your Silent Partner

Place your bed due north and south. At the very least, you will get a good night's sleep—and some people believe it will aid in the begetting of sons.

A Shopkeeper's Guide to Good Luck

There's an old superstition among merchants that in order to ensure good sales and good luck, you should spit on the first money taken in at the start of the day.

Some people also believe that you should then put it in a pocket all by itself, so it will draw money to itself.

If you make this first sale before 9 A.M. on a Monday, that's especially auspicious for the week ahead.

When starting up a new enterprise, leases for an odd number of months or years are lucky. That's why long-term leases run for 99 years, not 100 years.

Sign the lease on the third day of the waxing moon.

Open for business on the new moon.

"Entirely too much stress is put on the making of money. That does not require brains. Some of the biggest fools I know are the wealthiest. As a matter of fact, I believe that success is 95 percent luck and 5 percent ability. Take my own case. I know there are any number of men in my employ who could run my business just as well as I can. They didn't get the breaks—that's the only difference between them and me."

—*Julius Rosenwald,*
president of Sears, Roebuck
and Company, 1910–1925

Q: "How much of what you've done in your business career has been luck versus calculated risk?"

A: "If I told you it was all luck, I wouldn't be truthful. But if I told you it was all strategy, it would be a downright lie."

—John Werner Kluge,
one of the richest men in America,
in Electronic Media *magazine.*

How Mr. Rolls Met Mr. Royce

Early in this century, a manager of a machine shop in England was intensely interested in cars. His name was Mr. Rolls. He was trying to build a car that he could drive from home to work, a 32-mile trip, but the blasted thing just wouldn't run properly—perhaps, he finally concluded, because he was using such cheap materials. Finally he bit the bullet, ordered first-rate supplies, and built a car that ran like a top.

He also discovered that he'd ordered twice as much material as he needed. So he built a second car. Since he didn't need two cars, he sold the second one to a rich man named Mr. Royce. Mr. Royce loved the car so much he offered Mr. Rolls his backing. And the rest, as they say, is history . . .

"What numbers should you select? Actually, that's the wrong question—it should be what numbers shouldn't you select! This is because, being a greedy swine, you want all the money to yourself if you win the jackpot. So it's important to avoid 'obvious' numbers and sequences that other people might use . . .

"Once you've selected your numbers, stick with them! If you really must play around with a totally new set of numbers each week, keep your original set going as usual and buy a second ticket."

—*UK National Lottery Home Page*
(http://www.connect.org.uk/lottery)

"You gotta gamble
every now and
then. I might be
walking around a
lucky man and not
even know it!"

—*Lotto ticket buyer quoted in the*
Washington Post

Here's the Rub

Is it possible that good luck could literally "rub off"? Lottery winners often tell stories of being rubbed behind their ears, rubbed atop their heads—in some cases, people will literally rub elbows with them. It's one of the unexpected consequences of unexpectedly good luck.

One August morning in 1993, for example, Ed Gildein pulled up to the drive-in window at his local Dunkin' Donuts, bought an eclair and a lottery ticket—and won $8.9 million in the Texas Lottery. From then on, anytime he'd go out to dinner with his old friends the Scotts, Irene Scott would greet him by rubbing his back and saying, "I need some luck."

Twenty months later, the lucky rub paid off. Irene hit it big in the lottery for $2.2 million.

"After she won," says Ed, "everybody wanted to rub my back."

The Scotts are not alone, by the way. Others have won big after touching past winners for good luck. In Virginia, a tile installer named Andy Boehnlein was working on a new kitchen for a Virginia Lotto winner, hoping that the luck would rub off. It did, for $2.1 million. And in Illinois a bellman, Augustus Alvarez, won $2 million after he carried the suitcases of several folks attending the 1990 Illinois Lottery Millionaires Reunion. One of the millionaires told him, "It'll be your turn someday." A year later, it was.

If you rub a pair of dice on a red-headed person it will bring good luck. (To you, not them.)

The Luckiest of the Lucky: Repeat Lottery Winners

In 1985, a divorced convenience-store manager named Evelyn Marie Adams won $4 million in the New Jersey Lottery. Four months later she won another $1.5 million—and the proper authorities began poking around. There had to be some kind of shenanigans here, right? Nobody could be that lucky . . .

Yes, they could. Evelyn won fair and square, surmounting odds that were placed at something like 15 trillion to one. (To give you an idea how unlikely that is, 15 trillion is three thousand times the number of people on this planet.) Since then, others have joined the elite club of repeat winners. Among them:

❖ Randy Halvorson was one of 14 employees to win a $3.4 million jackpot in 1988. The

Iowa resident then won $7.2 million with his brother in 1990.

✤ Colorado resident Don Whitman, Jr., won $2 million in 1989 and another $2.2 million in 1991.

✤ John Martin became New York's first repeat winner in 1990, when he won an $800,000 share of a $4 million jackpot. He'd won $666,666 in 1986.

✤ Joseph P. Crowley won $3 million in the Ohio lottery in 1987. Six years later he retired to Boca Raton, Florida, and played the Florida Lotto on Christmas Day of 1993. He won $20 million.

✤ In Virginia, two people have won the state's $100,000 Cash 5 game twice: Helen Powell of Richmond and Kenneth D. Harris of Radford. The freaky thing about it is, they both won again on the same night: Monday, March 7, 1994.

It's gotten so that winning twice isn't astounding anymore. Believe it or not, there are now "threepeat" winners!

✤ In Massachusetts, Thomas M. Panagiotes won the Mass Cash game twice in 1993— on December 9th and again just three weeks later, on December 30th. He won it a third time on June 27, 1996. The game's prize: $100,000 per win.

✤ In Wisconsin, Donald Smith of Amherst has won the state's SuperCash game three times: On May 25, 1993, June 17, 1994, and July 30, 1995. He won $250,000 each time. The odds of winning the SuperCash game just once are nearly one in a million.

Old Voodoo Recipe for Gambling Luck

INGREDIENTS:
one small piece of chamois
one small piece of red flannel
one shark's tooth
sap from a pine tree
blood from a dove
cat's hair

Mix blood and sap together. Using this mixture, write your winning number or desired amount of winnings on the chamois. Lay the shark's tooth on it, cover with the red flannel, and sew together with cat's hair. Wear this in your left shoe.

"Life's one big, scary, glorious, complex and ultimately unfathomable crapshoot."

—The Badger *comic strip*

Bingo!

Americá's bingo halls are the friendly, come-as-you-are alternative to gambling casinos. Oh, they can't compete with the glitz and glamour of Las Vegas, they're about as hip as a Victrola, and the prize money is modest, at best. But by the same token, you can't gamble away your entire nest egg in a single night, and whatever you lose will fill the coffers of the local church, not a corporation traded on the New York Stock Exchange.

Which is why it's a $5 billion annual pastime.

Bingo players have a whole world of lucky charms unto themselves. Garfield dolls are popular charms, as are the California Raisins. Stuffed animals, especially teddy bears, are brought to the halls to bring luck. Figurines of monkeys are lucky; so are fig-

urines of elephants, but only if they're holding their trunks upward. And for some in-
scrutable reason, the big, big lucky charm
is—a troll.

Since bingo is habit-forming, it's easy to
do the same things at every game as a way to
woo Lady Luck. A devout player will sit in
the same seat, eat the same snack, buy cards
from the same cashier, use the same dauber
(card marker), and wear the same hat. As
luck would have it, the night's big winner has
probably worn the same muumuu to every
single game for two years now.

You Lucky Dog, You

Imagine having good luck give you a big sloppy kiss every time you walk through your door. Well, it can be arranged: just buy a Tibetan terrier.

These good-natured, long-haired little dogs, often likened to a miniature Old English Sheepdog, have been associated with good luck for over two thousand years. They were originally bred and raised only by lamas living in remote Tibetan monasteries in a place called the Lost Valley. It was "lost" in the 14th century, when an earthquake destroyed all access roads. After that, the valley was so inaccessible that visiting dignitaries or other visitors were often given one of these intelligent and companionable animals as a guide to lead them back to civilization.

Tibetan terriers came to be highly prized

as bringers of luck to their owners—they were the original "lucky dog." They were never sold because the Tibetans believed that to do so would be to sell away the owners' good fortune. As is true with many other lucky objects, they were only given as gifts. The breed was also kept pure for many generations, because cross-breeding a Tibetan terrier with any other sort of dog was thought to dilute their luckiness. The first time one of these faithful little dogs left Tibet was in the early 1920s, when a grateful Tibetan nobleman gave one to a British physician who had treated his sick wife. It wasn't until 1957 that the dogs reached the United States. Now Tibetan terriers are kept as devoted pets and exhibited in dog shows all over the world. They're still sometimes called by their ancient name, "Luck Bringers."

And perhaps they really are.

"Even the street dog has his lucky days."

—*Japanese saying*

Mascots

These days, team mascots are as entertaining as the sports franchises they work for. (Some nights, they're the only thrill.) They have names like Stuff the Magic Dragon, S.J. Sharkie, or, quite simply, Bear. They do crazy stunts, and generally act as cheerleader, jester, and fool.

All that is in addition to their traditional job description: a living, breathing good-luck charm.

The word "mascot" has its roots in the Provençal French words *masco*, or "witch," and *mascoto*, or "sorcery." It's a recent word in English, introduced by a French opera of 1880, *La Mascotte* (The Charm). It means something that brings good luck. The concept has been around awhile. Cats rode in Egyptian war chariots, leopards rode with Assyrian kings into battle, and every Roman legion had its eagle.

Of Black Cats and Good Luck

I f a black cat walks across your path, it's bad luck: That's probably one of the oldest and most widespread superstitions in the world.

But since ancient times black cats have also been associated with good luck. It's an old belief in Britain, for instance, that if a stray black cat walks into your house, that's a good omen. And rural fishermen in Yorkshire believed that keeping a black cat in the house would ensure the safety of husbands at sea. (This belief led to a lively black market in stolen black cats, which were then marketed to fishermen's wives.) King Charles I of Britain had a "lucky" black cat that he treasured so much that it was always carefully guarded. But one day it got sick and died. "My luck is gone!" the king moaned. Sure enough: He was arrested the next day, according to the historical record, and England's Civil War began.

Some writers have suggested that black-cat luck may have had its origin in ancient Egypt, where people worshipped a sacred black cat named Bast. During the reign of one early pharaoh, in fact, Bast became the official deity. And good luck always favored those who prayed to the gods and goddesses—even the feline versions.

Five Bats of Happiness

The *weefuh* is an ancient Chinese talisman with five bats in a circle. The five bats represent the five great sources of happiness in this life: luck, wealth, long life, health, and peace.

The Chinese, who have always been gracious about giving and receiving good luck, would use the *weefuh* to do just that. If you were a guest at someone's house for tea, you might empty your cup to see, printed on the bottom, a luck-wishing sentence such as, "May your happiness know no bounds." Surrounding it would be the five bats of happiness.

That's a Rap!

In Thailand, the nations most popular good-luck charm is a Buddhist monk named Luang Phor Khoon Parisuttho.

A few years ago, the monk gained a reputation for himself when worshippers who wore his amulets began surviving various calamities. For instance, one woman jumped from a fourth story window during a factory fire—and lived, she says, because she was wearing an amulet with his picture on it.

Now, every morning before dawn, people begin lining up outside his temple to receive his blessing. Rich and poor, old and young, even the Crown Princess has come by. Luang Phor Khoon treats all of them in the same manner. He sits cross-legged on a dais and, as his supplicants file past, he swats them on the head with a rolled-up newspaper. Sometimes luck works in strange ways.

The Seven Gods
of Luck

In Western culture, luck is often depicted as a woman. But "Lady Luck" is just one way of imagining the force of chance in human life. For instance, one favorite theme of Japanese folk tales are the Seven Gods of Luck *(Shichi-fuku-jin)*, whimsical deities associated with good fortune and happiness. They're often shown on their treasure ship together with various magical implements, such as a hat of invisibility, rolls of brocade, an inexhaustible purse, keys to the divine treasure house, cloves, scrolls or books, a lucky rain hat, and a robe of feathers.

The Seven Gods of Luck came to have great appeal in the 17th and 18th centuries, particularly among the merchant classes. But even today in Japan, it's quite common to make a New Year's pilgrimage to a series of shrines and temples associated with them. Particularly popular is the custom of placing a picture of the seven, aboard their treasure ship, beside one's pillow on New Year's Eve to guarantee that the first dream of the year will be a lucky one.

"Starting with my mother, who was an actress, just about every performer I have known has been at least mildly superstitious."

—*Nancy Reagan,* My Turn

What the Stars Did for Luck on Opening Night

❖ Have someone give you a red apple. (John, Ethel, and Lionel Barrymore always did that for each other.)

❖ Touch every lamppost on your way to the theater. (Don Fellows)

❖ Get sick. (Alec Guinness would get horrible pains in his knees and back.)

❖ Convince yourself that everyone in the audience is a personal friend of yours. (José Ferrer)

❖ Have someone write you a poem, and be sure they deliver it to the theater. (Walter McGinn)

❖ Wear old clothes. (Al Jolson)

❖ Wear old shoes. (Ed Wynn wore the same pair for 20 years.)

❖ Kiss all your lucky charms just before going onstage. (Wilfrid Hyde White)

"You name it, honey, I believe in it."

—*Tallulah Bankhead,*
American actress

More Superstitions of the Stage

❖ If your shoes squeak, that's good luck.

❖ If you kick off your shoes and they alight on their soles, that's also good luck.

❖ If you should fall flat on your face when making your entrance, that's spectacular luck.

❖ All wigs are lucky.

❖ If you get a first-night telegram, burn the envelope.

❖ Make sure there's soap in your dressing room.

❖ In every rehearsal, stop short of saying the final lines of the script.

❖ If the first person to buy tickets is elderly, that signifies a long, lucky run.

❖ Touch the curtain when it finally comes down. For some reason, you'll get better reviews if you do.

✤ Don't knit onstage or open an umbrella onstage. Never whistle in the dressing room.

✤ Above all, don't say the word "Macbeth."
   Say "the Scottish play" or simply refer to it
   as "that play."

"Everybody wants good luck and dreads bad luck, but in few people is the desire so urgent or the fear so passionate as in an actor facing his nightly ordeal."

—*Richard Huggett,*
Supernatural on Stage

Lucky Nights at the Opera

The German operatic composer Richard Wagner used to kneel down and kiss the stage floor.

Jacques Offenbach, the French composer of operettas, had a unique lucky charm—a baton carved from a croupier's rake. It had been given to him once at a casino in Baden-Baden where he spent a very lucky night winning a pile of money. The baton lay on his piano when he was composing, and he wrote all his best-known work after he acquired it.

Italian tenor Luigi Ravelli always sang to his dog in his dressing room before a performance. Enrico Caruso carried a ring strung with charms in the pocket of his costumes; his valet's chief duty was to make sure the

ring was in a pocket at every performance.
And modern tenor Luciano Pavarotti always
picks up a bent nail as a keepsake—the "V"
being an old good-luck sign.

In Sweden, opera stars are given a kick
in the rear for good luck just before walking
on stage. French opera stars spit and say,
"merde, merde, merde" before making their
entrances.

The famous Victorian team of Gilbert
and Sullivan got launched one night when a
Japanese ceremonial sword, which hung
above Gilbert's fireplace, fell down with a
bang on a windy day. It triggered a series of
ideas, which led to *The Mikado*. The next
decade brought forth their best work, and
the sword was placed above Gilbert's desk.
Then one night thieves stole it—and their
fortunes ended. They wrote only one more
opera, *The Grand Duke*, and that was a dis-
aster.

Good-Luck Charms from the Golden Age of the Silver Screen

1. Alfred Hitchcock was his own lucky charm—he made brief appearances in all his films for good luck, not vanity.

2. Joan Crawford kept a red belt in her dressing room—she'd worn it in the play *The Guardsman* early in her career.

3. Greta Garbo had a lucky rope of pearls.

4. Humphrey Bogart had a silver cocktail shaker, five German helmets, and an Egyptian scarab.

5. Bette Davis also had a golden scarab.

6. Carole Lombard kept a smooth, round pebble given to her by Clark Gable.

7. Cecil B. De Mille wore lucky riding breeches to work.

8. John Wayne had a living good-luck charm: Ward Bond. Wayne made sure Bond appeared in all his films.

9. Jack Lemmon whispered the words "magic time" just before the cameras began to roll.

10. Tallulah Bankhead always kept a hare's foot given to her by her father in 1936. At her funeral it was placed in her coffin.

The Rabbit's Foot

Suppose you were a poor peasant living in Europe a couple thousand years ago. The world had far fewer people back then, but a lot more animals. Animals impressed you. Some of them could do things you couldn't, and some even seemed to know things you didn't.

Imagine what you might think about an animal with these characteristics:

✦ On moonlit nights it gathers in groups to engage in strange, silent play;

✦ It thumps the ground with its hind feet, as if sending messages to spirits in the earth;

✦ It's incredibly prolific—it breeds faster than any other mammal;

✦ When it runs, its hind feet hit the ground in front of its forefeet. Only two other animals, the greyhound and the cheetah, can do that—and if you were a poor European peasant, you never heard of either;

✦ It's fast as lightning. And clever to boot, so that it outwits the finest hunters.

No wonder the rabbit—and its European cousin the hare—has assumed magical properties. Imagine if you could get your hands on one of those powerful hind feet, and do it by the light of a full moon, no less. Then you'd have some of that power—because back then magic was believed to be "contagious." Part of a thing possesses the properties of the whole, even after contact is severed. Yes, even at a distance they share a secret empathy.

Long ago the rabbit's foot was probably a charm meant to confer sexual powers and fertility. It evolved into a talisman with healing powers: It could cure afflictions of the foot, like gout, and all forms of rheumatism. In the 17th century English diarist Samuel Pepys believed that touching a rabbit's foot cured his indigestion. "Strange how fancy works," he wrote afterward, "for I had no sooner handled his foot but I became well and so continue."

Today it has become a charm conferring good luck in general, rather than any benefit in particular. Admiral George Dewey wore a rabbit's foot in the Battle of Manila Bay in the Spanish-American War of 1898; afterward he sent it to a friend in New Jersey, who placed it on exhibit, thus helping to popularize the charm in America. A couple of generations ago, rabbit's feet were in every corner drugstore; millions were sold each year. Their popularity has waned, but they are still sold as key chains. And some actors, we're told, use a rabbit's foot to put on makeup. It's a way to wish yourself good luck in a profession so superstitious, it's bad luck to wish someone, "Good luck!"

When "Good Luck" Is Not

Don't ever wish a performer, "Good luck." That's very bad luck. Say, instead, "Break a leg." Or simply wish them well.

The wit Dorothy Parker may have come up with the raciest of theatrical salutations when she sent a telegram to actress Uta Hagen saying, "A hand on your opening and may your parts grow bigger."

Are You the Son of a White Hen?

The ancient Romans used the expression "son of a white hen" to describe anyone who enjoyed good luck. If it sounds like there's a story behind that, you're right. The second-century historian Suetonius relates the following: One day, shortly after her marriage to Emperor Augustus, Livia was returning to her villa near Veii. An eagle, flying by, dropped a white hen that was carrying a laurel twig. It fell right into her lap. What an omen! (The Romans loved omens.) She raised the hen and planted the laurel twig. The twig grew into a tree; that tree was used by the Caesars to provide laurel wreaths for their triumphs.

If you were a Roman, you grew up knowing that story. And so the expression made perfect sense. Good luck, like the Empress Livia's white hen, simply drops out of the sky one day. And falls right in your lap.

"Good fortune, like ripe fruit, ought to be enjoyed while it is present."

—*Epictetus*

The Goddess of Luck

The ancient Romans worshipped many gods and goddesses, but one of the leading deities was the goddess of luck. Her name was Fortuna—which is where we get our word "fortune" as a synonym for fate or destiny. (The Latin root word, *forte*, means "by chance" or "accidentally.")

The goddess Fortuna was immensely popular. So all-encompassing were her powers, Romans would build shrines to just one aspect of her. There were shrines to men's fortune and women's fortune; shrines to virgin fortune and the return of good fortune. The Greek philosopher Plutarch, writing about Roman life in the first century A.D., noted drily, "Even now they have no temple of Wisdom or Prudence or Constancy or Magnanimity. But of Fortune there are very many ancient and splendid temples . . . interspersed throughout the most conspicuous districts and localities of the City." Here all citizens, but particularly married women, would pray for good luck in their daily affairs.

Part of her popularity is explained by the ancient Roman view of fate. One's lot in life seemed capricious. And as Rome reached its height, enormous (and carelessly abused) power was concentrated at the center of the Empire, while dangers lurked at the edges. Yes, the good times rolled—and often they rolled right over you. Every Roman felt that life wasn't very fair; the goddess Fortuna represented a useful, if flippant, summary of the way things go.

Fortuna was commonly depicted holding a cornucopia (horn of plenty). An apt symbol when you consider that she was the one who handed out life's riches. She also held a rudder—for it was she who steered people's destinies. Often she was standing on a ball to show the uncertainty of her appearances. By the medieval era, this ball became a wheel—an ever-turning wheel to show that people's fortunes rise and fall, so it is wise not to depend on fortune when you're up, nor to despair of it when you're down.

"Throughout the whole world, in all places and at all times, Fortuna alone is invoked, alone commended, alone accused and subjected to reproaches; deemed volative and indeed, by most men, blind as well, wayward, capricious, fickle in her favors and favoring the unworthy. To her is debited all that is spent, and to her is credited all that is received; she alone fills both pages in the ledger of mortals' accounts; and we are so subject to chance that Chance herself takes the place of God; she proves that God is uncertain."

—*Pliny the Elder,* Natural History

Hail, Caesar! Luckiest of Men!

Most corporate CEOs and elected officials don't go around proclaiming their good luck. They'd rather die than say such a thing. Our culture, after all, honors pluck instead of luck. But this was not always and everywhere the case. A leader wanted to be perceived as lucky, because his leadership took on an aura of destiny from it. And many a nation wanted its leader to be lucky—for if Fortune smiled upon him, her blessings would also shine down upon his people. Or so they hoped.

A paramount example of the lucky leader is Julius Caesar. Born in the year 100 B.C., he will always be remembered as the man at the center of Rome's transformation from republic to empire. The month July is named after him; his family name of Caesar has meant "maximum leader" for 2,000 years; he dated Cleopatra. Very impressive.

Caesar always admitted that he became Rome's first emperor because of good luck. In fact, he bragged about it. All of Rome was convinced he'd succeeded because of good fortune, noted the first-century biographer Plutarch. In fact, there's a story in Plutarch's *Moralia*, that illustrates it beautifully.

Before he'd consolidated his power, Caesar ruled for ten years in a triumvirate with Pompey and Crassus. This arrangement was doomed to fail. Finally, Caesar had to do battle with a much more popular and powerful Pompey. So on the fourth of January, 49 B.C., he and his troops set out across the Mediterranean to meet the foe in Spain. Though it was winter, he crossed the sea in safety; "Fortune postponed the season," says Plutarch. When he got there, he found that Pompey had a bigger army on land, a bigger fleet on the sea, and was well entrenched.

Caesar's allies at that time, Mark Anthony and Sabinus, were slow in coming, so Caesar got into a small boat and put out to sea, disguised as a servant and unrecognized by the pilot. When they came to the mouth of a river, the sea suddenly surged, and the pilot started to turn back. Caesar then threw the cloak off his head and said, "Go on, good sir, and fear nothing! But entrust your sails to Fortune and receive her breeze, confident because you bear Caesar and Caesar's Fortune."

In the end, says Plutarch, "Fortune's task it was to enjoin calm upon the sea, summer weather upon the winter-time, speed upon the slowest of men, courage upon the most dispirited, and (more unbelievable than these) to enjoin flight upon Pompey." It was Fortune who lifted up Caesar and cast down his rivals, leaving him to rule alone.

"Superstition
is a quality
that seems
indigenous
to the ocean."

—*James Fenimore Cooper*

Luck at Sea

Anyone who goes down to the sea in ships faces danger and uncertainty. No wonder sailors are the most superstitious people on earth. Any number of things can cause bad luck, seamen believe (changing a ship's name, for instance, or bringing flowers aboard). But plenty of other things attract good luck to seamen and their ships.

Many vessels have bare-breasted women as figureheads because there's an ancient belief that a naked woman can cause gales to subside. To sailors, a woman in her altogether is the ultimate good-luck charm.

Nailing a horseshoe to the mast ensures good luck. And when the ship is built, the mast should rest upon a silver coin.

Christening a ship with a bottle of champagne descends from the ancient idea that the gods of the sea must be propitiated, that is, wooed for good luck. The ancient Greeks used wine or oil, but sometimes blood from a human sacrifice. In fact, before champagne became popular in modern times, blood-red wine was often used.

Since ancient times, seamen have worn gold earrings, not only because they look dashing but also because they're lucky charms against drowning.

Other Seafaring Beliefs

✤ Sailors, like many other people, believe that odd numbers are lucky. That's why nearly all maritime gun salutes (the most famous of which is the 21-gun salute) are composed of an odd number of explosions.

✤ There's a widespread belief that if you see a sailor, touching his collar is good luck.

✤ An old tradition among seamen says that Sunday is a lucky day to begin a voyage or to go fishing, but Friday is not. In Welsh folklore, Friday is the day the fairies rule the sea, making it rough and stormy. Hence the old sailor's ditty:

> *Sunday sail, never fail.*
> *Friday sail, ill luck and gale.*

✤ If you're becalmed in a sailing vessel, try whistling; it's said to bring wind. Otherwise, it's bad luck to whistle on board a ship because it's likely to bring on gales.

✤ Most seabirds that follow ships—gulls, storm petrels, and especially the albatross—are associated with good luck. They're said to be the spirits of drowned sailors, and should never be harmed. Some sailors even believe it's especially good luck if a bird defecates on you at sea.

A Lucky Life Preserver

One of the oldest and most powerful of sailors' lucky charms is the caul, or the amniotic sac that surrounds a fetus in the womb. Normally the sac bursts shortly before childbirth—it's said that the mother's "water breaks"—but very rarely are children born "in caul," meaning that they're still inside the unbroken sac. Because it's almost as if these special children are able to live underwater, sailors have long prized the remnants of a child's caul as a lucky charm against drowning.

Scottish fishermen called the lucky caul a "silly-hoo" or a "hally-how"; others call it a "happy hood." It was often sewn into a sailors' clothing and worn for the entire length of a voyage, in hopes that it would protect both ship and sailor .

"Throw a lucky man into the sea, and he will come up with a fish in his mouth."

—*Arab proverb*

Lucky Lindy's Favorite Charm

No one can resist picking up an odd-looking pebble while strolling along the beach; a strange, smooth stone tucked in a pocket must be the oldest lucky charm in the world.

But far from the ocean, in the Blue Ridge Mountains of southwest Virginia, are 50 acres on top of Bull Mountain in Patrick County, where you'll find some of the world's oddest stones. They've come to be called Virginia fairy crosses, or fairy stones, and they've been associated with good luck for as long as anybody can remember. It's not hard to understand why: They're dark brown or whitish, an inch or two long, formed in the shape of perfect, tiny crosses. They look almost precisely like a crucifix made of stone, with edges so precisely beveled they look machine-made. But it was the hand of nature that made them.

Thousands of people around the world have carried them as amulets against disease, misfortune, and danger, in lockets, as watch charms, as jewelry, or simply as pocket tokens that can be rubbed for luck. In fact, the Virginia fairy cross was the favorite lucky charm of three U.S. presidents—Theodore Roosevelt, Woodrow Wilson, and Warren G. Harding. The great inventor Thomas Edison and Charles "Lucky" Lindbergh, the celebrated flier who first crossed the Atlantic alone, were also known to carry these lucky stones.

Of the many legends that have attached to fairy stones, one of the loveliest refers to a time almost two thousand years ago, when fairies were said to cavort through the mountain glades of the Blue Ridge. One day, while they were dancing with the wood nymphs around a cool spring, an elfin messenger came from a faraway city bringing tidings of the death of Christ. When the fairies heard the news of his crucifixion, they wept. As their tears fell upon the earth, they turned into sparkling pebbles in the form of tiny crosses. When the fairies disappeared with the coming of civilization, it's said, the mountaintop was still strewn with their crystalline tears.

Some people still call fairy crosses "tears." Geologists call them staurolite crystals, a word derived from *staurus* ("cross") and *lite* ("stone"); they're made of a dark silicate of aluminum and iron. But then, geology is never quite as satisfying as poetry.

"Greater qualities are necessary to bear good fortune than bad."

—*La Rochefoucauld*

The Luck of Eden Hall

One night, in an England of long, long ago, a group of fairies were gathered around St. Cuthbert's Well in Cumberland. They were in the midst of drinking and making merry when they were surprised by the butler of nearby Eden Hall. They ran off, leaving a drinking cup at the well's edge. The last fairy to depart shouted over its shoulder:

> *If this cup should break or fall*
> *Farewell the Luck of Eden Hall!*

The story may not be real, but the cup is very real. It's a painted glass goblet of Syrian workmanship dating back to the early 1200s—in other words, an item undoubtedly brought back from one of the later Crusades. And it has belonged to the Musgrave family for as long as they've owned the estate called Eden Hall—which is since the middle of the 1400s. For five centuries the Musgraves have prospered, married well, and held offices of importance. And they believe they owe their remarkable family continuity to their continuous care of the cup.

Most lucky objects are held by individuals; they are not meant to be communal, and certainly not hereditary. But on the British Isles the landed gentry came to venerate certain family heirlooms as being actually magical. So long as those "lucks" are safe and sound, the family and its fortunes are safe and sound. In the late sixteenth century, such objects became a cult, when the nouveau riche, as eager then as today to make their new money seem like old money, obtained objects and dressed up their provenance with a bit of rich lore. By the time of the "Gothick Revival" of the eighteenth century, when England became utterly fascinated with its medieval past, many if not most of the ancient families of Britain had something—a sword, a banner, a goblet, or a trumpet—upon which they swore the well-being of their house depended. About that time, a ballad was written in honor of the Luck of Eden Hall, and it quickly became the most famous object of its kind in Britain.

Some "lucks" are not as old or renowned as the family would have us believe, but others plainly date back to the late Middle Ages. At that time, most nobles could not read, and so there was little use for a deed to hand down property. Instead, the king would give a sword or goblet as a tangible emblem of the estates he gave away. Quite literally, the possession of a family's lands and castle depended on that object. And that may well have been the original purpose of the Musgraves' "luck": it granted them tenure to Eden Hall. That it has done, and more.

"Luck stops at the door and inquires whether Prudence is within."

—*Danish proverb*

A Russian Folk Tale

Once there were two brothers. One was rich, and one was poor—so poor he had only one horse to plow his field, and that one died. In desperation he asked his rich brother to lend him a horse for just one day. At first his brother refused, but the poor brother pleaded until he relented.

The poor brother went to the rich brother's field to find a horse. There he saw a strong man plowing his brother's field.

"Who are you?" asked the poor man.

"I am your brother's Good Luck," said the strong man. "I make sure your brother prospers."

"What about my Good Luck?" asked the poor man.

"There is your Good Luck," said the strong man, pointing to a little toothpick of a lad sleeping underneath a tree. The poor man woke him up with a hard pinch. The poor man's Good Luck refused to plow the fields like the rich man's Good Luck. "But here's what I can do," he said. "I'll help you to engage in trade."

So after discussing things with Good Luck, the poor brother and his family packed their things and set off for town. As they were packing, they heard the sound of weeping. It was Bad Luck, crying because he was being left behind. The poor brother told Bad Luck he could come to town only if he jumped into an old sack. The trick worked and the poor brother dug a hole beside his old hut and buried the bag.

Once in town, according to the plan, the poor brother sold his wife's old dress for a small sum. With that he bought one a little better, which he sold for a little more. And so it went until, gradually, the poor man became rich.

In time his rich brother heard the news

and came to town to see for himself. Indeed, he saw that his formerly poor brother was now richer than he.

"Your family was starving!" he said. "How did you get rich?"

"I put Bad Luck in a bag and buried it," said the newly rich brother, laughing beside the old hut.

The rich brother quickly said good-bye and started home. On the way, his heart grew bitter with jealousy and spite. He went straight to his brother's old hut and dug up the bag. He untied the knot and set Bad Luck free.

"Go find my brother," he cried. "Take his wealth!"

"Oh, no!" said Bad Luck. "I'd rather stay with you."

"Many a stroke of luck has come to many a hopeless man."

—*Plautus, Roman dramatist*

An Aesop Fable

Two men were traveling together along a road. Suddenly one of them stopped and picked up a purse. Someone had lost it on the way.

"Look what I have found!" he cried. "It is very heavy! It must be full of money."

Quickly he opened it. "How lucky I am!" he said when he saw that it was full of gold.

"You should say how lucky WE are," his companion said. "Aren't we traveling together? Travelers should share both their good luck and their bad."

"No, indeed!" the other said. "I found it and I am going to keep it."

He had no sooner said this than they heard a cry of "Stop, thief!" They looked behind them. A mob of people was surging toward them. And everyone in that mob was armed with a heavy stick.

The traveler who had picked up the purse grew pale with fright.

"We are lost if they find the purse upon us!" he cried. "They will think we stole it!"

But his companion did not share his fright. "Don't say WE are lost," he said. "You would not say 'we' before. So now say I am lost."

Moral: If you do not share your good fortune with others, do not expect them to share in your misfortunes.

"True luck consists not in the holding the best of the cards at the table:

Luckiest he who knows just when to rise and go home."

—John Hay,
American statesman

"I must complain the cards are ill-shuffled, till I have a good hand."

—*Jonathan Swift,*
English satirist

"Fortuna takes away nothing that she hasn't already given."

—*Seneca*

Truly a Fortune Cookie

Fortune cookies carry lottery numbers on the back of the little slip of paper that's supposed to foretell your destiny. This has prompted many a diner, while lingering over an unfinished pu-pu platter, to ask: Has anyone actually won a lottery using these numbers? The answer is yes. Several times. In fact, three people once won the Texas lottery after eating at the same restaurant chain.

In March of 1995, Barbara and Scott Turnbull got a fortune cookie at a China Coast restaurant in the southern Texas town of McAllen. They both bought tickets with the same numbers—and won $814,000 each.

Meanwhile, up in northern Texas, Nealy LaHair got a fortune cookie with the same numbers from a China Coast restaurant in Dallas. She played the numbers, and won a $814,000 share of the jackpot for herself.

Luck some-
times visits
a fool, but
never sits
down with
him.

—*German proverb*

Seven Time-Honored Ways to Change Your Luck at the Card Table

1. Ask for a new deck.

2. Blow on the cards.

3. Sit on a handkerchief, unfolded into a square.

4. Circle the table three times, left to right.

5. Turn your chair around three times.

6. Turn the back of your chair to the table and straddle it.

7. "Cross out" your opponent's luck by placing matchsticks in the form of a cross on the table.

"Look you:
How excellent
a thing is
Chance!"

—*Alexandre Dumas,*
The Three Musketeers

OPRAH WINFREY:
"Do you think this happened for a reason?"

PAM BARTON (WHO WON $10 MILLION IN A PUBLISHER'S SWEEPSTAKES IN 1993):
"You know, I tried to make sense of it for a while. But it just doesn't make any sense."

OPRAH WINFREY:
"Then it doesn't make sense."

PAM BARTON:
"It's just lucky."

—The Oprah Winfrey Show

"Anyone is potentially a recipient of luck. If I fancy myself winning in competition with a master player of tennis or chess, I am an idiot—in view of my lack of the requisite skills. But if I envision winning a lottery, I am no more foolish than anybody else. Anyone can carry off the prize here, and any person's chance of winning is just as good as anyone else's. Gambling of this sort is, in a way, a great equalizer."

—*Nicolas Rescher,* Luck: The Brilliant Randomness of Everyday Life

"For me dumb luck overcomes dumbness."

—*Bill Mayhew,*
$2 million Maryland
lottery winner

"Regardless of the system you use, you've got to be lucky to win. It's just pure luck."

—*Sam Valenza, Jr.*,
Lottery & Casino News

Lucky Hunches

Almost everybody has had a fleeting intuition that something is going to happen, or that some action should be taken—and it's turned out to be eerily accurate. It's called a "lucky hunch."

But why do we call them "hunches"?

The reason is that, since very ancient times, people with hunchbacks have been associated with good luck. However mistakenly, this may have to do with the worldwide belief that grotesque or devil-like images will scare off the spirits they're supposed to represent. That's why medieval churches all over Europe have leering gargoyles on their roofs—the uglier the better. Or maybe it's because hunchbacks, like many other things thought to be bizarre or peculiar, evoke a kind of primitive awe and wonder. As if they're linked to some powerful, mysterious magic.

For whatever reason, seeing—or even touching—a hunchback has long been thought to increase one's luck. The Egyptians worshipped a hunchbacked god named Bes. In Roman times, nobles would employ hunchbacks as a way of blessing their households with luck. The less-well-off tended to favor small images of hunchbacks called "gobbos," fashioned of metal, wood, or stone. These lucky charms have been found around the world. Phoenician sailors, setting off on long voyages, would take along a gobbo to protect them at sea. A century ago at Monte Carlo, gamesters believed that if they touched their gobbo, good luck was a sure thing.

FILM CONTRACT

Good Luck,
If Not Good Looks

In the region of England called Northumberland, there's an old tradition that if you have a gap between your front teeth, you'll be lucky and travel. (It certainly hasn't hurt David Letterman's career.)

In the British Midlands, people with lots of hair on their hands and arms are said to be "born to be rich."

If you've got fleshy webs between your toes, like a frog or a duck, you're not strange—you're lucky. According to an old Scottish belief, people with webbed toes will have good luck all their life. In fact, those lucky-duck tootsies are known as "lucken toes."

My, What Big Ears You Have!

Excessive luckiness has been associated with all sorts of body parts in various cultures around the world. In Japan, for instance, good luck is associated with big ears. The whimsical good-luck charms of Japanese folklore, The Seven Gods of Luck, are often depicted as having enormous, droopy ears—sometimes almost as big as a donkey's. And Buddha statues, you may have noticed, very often have enormous earlobes. (Rubbing a Buddha's rotund belly is said to be lucky, too.)

"The more you know, the more luck you will have."

—*Confucius*

"The harder you work, the luckier you get."

—*Gary Player, pro golfer*

"You hear it said that people make their own luck. But if you take 'luck' to mean chance events, happenstance, then the statement isn't true. Luck happens to everybody. You don't make your own luck. It comes and goes on its own. But you can make your own fortune, by staying alert and using luck wisely."

—*Charles Evan Cardwell*

The Night They
Invented Champagne

Humans stumbled upon the secrets of wine making many thousands of years ago—but champagne's story is only about 300 years old. The man generally credited with being its inventor was a French monk named Pierre Perignon—Dom Perignon.

Perignon was born in 1638, and entered holy orders at age 19. By age 30, he was appointed cellar master at the Benedictine Abbey of Hautvillers in the Champagne region of France. There he refined several wine-making techniques, including the blending of wines and the use of cork stoppers.

The wines of the Champagne region were slightly fizzy before Perignon came along—in the spring following the harvest, they'd produce a spritz on the tongue called *petillance* that resulted from fermentation in the casks over the preceding months. But it was a short-lived effect. What was needed, to make reliable bubbly, was a switch from cask fermentation to fermentation in bottles, plus the use of strong corks—so that when fermentation produced carbon dioxide, the gas would be forced to dissolve in the wine and make it sparkle.

Whether Perignon set out deliberately to enhance and prolong the natural *petillance* is not known. No conclusive records have survived from the late 1600s, when the champagnes of Champagne first burst upon the scene. Was it luck on his part—or merely on ours? We are left only with a legend that hints at the role of chance. It is said that when the blind Perignon sampled the very first successful bottle, he shouted to his fellow monks, "Brothers, come quickly! I am drinking stars!"

"Fortune is the arbiter of half the things we do, leaving the other half or so to be controlled by ourselves."

—*Niccolo Machiavelli*, The Prince

"Even a blind pig finds an acorn sometimes."

—President Bill Clinton,
exulting after finally
breaking 80 in a
round of golf.

"It's hard to detect good luck—it looks so much like something you've earned."

—*Frank A. Clark,*
"The Country Parson"

Luck, the Hidden Asset

"Most businessmen, I have discovered, possess two sets of opinions on the matter. One is for private, the other for public use—for consumption in plant bulletins, trade-journal interviews, Rotary Club orations, and inspirational school deliverances. This latter brand of philosophy deals in such uplifting phrases as 'Pluck makes Luck,' 'The wise man is a maker of opportunities,' 'Every man is the architect of his own fortune.' Many a man has one of these bromidic mottoes hanging above his desk—and a cherished lucky-piece hanging from his vest!"

—*John T. Flynn,* Harper's Weekly

How Do You Think They Got So Rich?

Why are some people so darn good at making money? Is there something different about them—and if so, what? That's got to be one of the biggest mysteries of all time. Every generation ponders the issue anew, so in the early 1970s a group of social scientists at Harvard thought they'd take a crack at it. Led by sociologist Christopher Jencks, they looked at census data and a 20-year study that followed the progress of 5,000 families in order to trace the roots of economic success.

Jencks and his team looked at the factors that are commonly suspected: People who earn the most had a proper upbringing, or were sent to all the right schools, or always scored well on early I.Q. tests or college entrance exams, or they had an inside track on the right occupations—like bond trading. Jencks's conclusion: Phooey. Those things don't matter all that much.

So what does matter? On-the-job competence—that is, how well you do whatever you've chosen to do. And luck. In fact, they concluded, "We suspect that luck has at least as much effect as competence on income."

That's a conclusion that many people—especially successful people—would resist, and Jencks's team knew it. "Those who are lucky tend, of course, to impute their success to skill, while those who are inept believe that they are merely unlucky," they wrote in their book, *Inequality: A Reassessment of the Effect of Family and Schooling in America.* "If one man makes money speculating in real estate while another loses it, the former will credit his success to good judgment while the latter will blame his failure on bad luck. So, too, if a worker's firm expands rapidly and promotes him, he will assume this is a tribute to his foresight in picking the right firm and his talent on the job. If his firm goes broke and leaves him with an unmarketable set of specialized skills, he will seldom blame himself. In general, we think luck has far more influence on income than successful people admit."

I Was Walking Down the Street One Day . . .

Every prosperous businessperson who's honest enough to be humble would have to admit that luck has played some role in his or her success.

Take Barnett Helzberg, Jr. He likes to tell the story of one of his luckiest breaks, which took place on a New York City street corner one summer morning in 1994.

WATERWORKS | PARK AVENUE

Helzberg was walking down the street that day when he heard someone call out

"Mr. Buffett!" to a man next to him.

Helzberg had never seen Warren Buffett, but he'd read all about him—Buffett was the second richest man in America. In fact, Helzberg owned stock in Buffett's company, Berkshire Hathaway. And since Helzberg was an avid reader of Buffett's famously wry comments in the annual reports, he also knew about the financial criteria Buffett used when he considered buying a company.

It just so happened that Helzberg also knew his own company—Helzberg Diamond Shops, the third-largest jewelry chain in the U.S.—perfectly fit the bill. As luck would have it, Helzberg had also recently turned 60 and was considered selling his company. He couldn't think of a more perfect buyer than Warren Buffett.

So when Helzberg overheard the woman call out Buffett's name on that street corner in New York, he seized the moment. As he later described it, "I walked over to Buffett, and we had a very detailed 20-second meeting."

In May of 1995, Buffett bought Helzberg Diamond Shops, a chain of 164 stores with annual revenues of around $300 million.

That deal would never have happened if Helzberg hadn't been walking down that street, or if that woman hadn't called out Buffett's name.

Thirty seconds either way and that meeting never would have happened.

"What makes a superstar is luck. None of those [very wealthy] guys is that smart."

—*Dennis Washington,
highway construction mogul
(and very wealthy guy)*

"Just choosing to work on Wall Street in the early Eighties—now, that was lucky."

—*David Wittig*

"I always knock on wood before I make my entrance."

—*Will Rogers*

Why We
Knock on Wood

K nocking on wood is one of those superstitions with a direct line of descent from our pagan past. In virtually every culture, on every continent, trees were worshipped. Early on they were regarded as animate objects with souls of their own. Later they were believed to be dwelling places of lesser gods who could exert their powers over spring rains, the growth of crops—and human fertility as well. In England, France, and Germany, various maypole customs came down from the tree worship of Celtic and Teutonic ancestors.

So did the custom of knocking on wood—or if you're British, touching it—when mentioning your own good luck.

Exactly what effect would this have?

There are two theories. One is that the rapping represents a toned-down version of the ruckus once raised in order to chase away evil spirits—or to prevent them from hearing a boast. (If they heard, they would try to do what evil beings always do: spoil whatever's good.) The other theory is that, by touching the wood, you are performing the modern version of an ancient rite: propitiating the spirit in the tree. Once upon a time, people actually touched the bark of a tree when requesting a favor of the good spirit within; if it was granted, they would return and touch the tree again to show gratitude.

In either case, you are seeking protection against envy and anger—the envy of evil spirits, and the anger of the gods, who take a dim view of mortals bearing too much pride, and who get especially annoyed when they're responsible for your run of luck and you're not grateful.

Does this quirky little action really come

straight from our tree-worshipping ancestors? Is that just too preposterous? Perhaps—but not to knock on wood is even more preposterous. When we knock on wood after boasting, we narrowly escape being braggarts. We show some humility. We are acknowledging that we are not all-powerful; we are not grabbing all the credit for our good fortune. Good luck has played a part. To imply otherwise would be both arrogant and stupid, and would inflame envy and anger in our listeners.

Believe what you will about the origins; knocking on wood still serves an ancient purpose.

Gardener's Luck

According to old English tradition, two kinds of garden oddities are signs of good luck:

✤ A peapod with only one pea in it.

✤ A "double cabbage" (one with two shoots coming out of the root instead of one).

Pennsylvania Dutch Rules for a Prosperous Harvest

✤ Don't plant peas or beans on the same day that baking is done.

✤ Plant peas and potatoes when the corners of the moon are up (i.e., waxing).

✤ If a pregnant woman helps to plant a fruit tree, and if she takes hold of it with both hands, the tree will bear doubly well.

✤ If you want big cucumbers, have a man plant them.

The Four-Leaf Clover

Four-leaf clovers are thought to be lucky throughout Europe and North America. The Druids believed that whoever found a four-leaf clover would be granted special power to see witches and evil spirits who roam the world unseen in order to provoke mischief and misery. Lucky the person, indeed, who can see evil in disguise!

Its value as a charm once depended in part on its rarity—it's a mutation on the normal three-lobed variety. Nowadays a four-leaf clover is not so rare and wonderful: horticulturalists have bred the strain.

If you should find one growing in your lawn or garden, keep it with you—don't give it away, or you'll bring bad luck on yourself. And wish for truth in the old saying:

> *One leaf for fame,*
> *One leaf for wealth,*
> *And one leaf for a faithful lover,*
> *And one leaf to bring glorious health*
> *Are all in a four-leaf clover!*

More Fisherman's Luck

There's a tradition among fishermen that, to ensure good luck, you should throw back the first fish that you catch—perhaps to appease the water spirits. Some fishermen also believe it's good luck to spit on the bait or to put a lucky coin in the boat.

Lightning Only Strikes . . . Seven Times

The number seven has always been regarded as lucky. Especially by Roy C. Sullivan.

According to the *Guinness Book of Records*, Sullivan holds the distinction of having been struck by lightning more often than anyone on the planet—and living to tell about it. A former park ranger, he started taking his hits in 1942, when he lost his big toenail. He wasn't hit again until 1969, when he lost his eyebrows, but then got hit in 1970 (left shoulder seared), in 1972 (hair set on fire), in 1973 (hair set on fire again! Hate when that happens!), and in 1976 (ankle injured). His seventh death-defying hit happened the following year, in 1977, when he suffered chest and stomach burns while fishing. And that was no fish story.

The Longest Fall

Is there anything worse than getting struck by lightning? Yes: being on an airplane that blows up. And yet, for Vesna Vulovic, enough good luck came along to change her fate.

In 1972, Vulovic was a 22-year-old flight attendant on a Yugoslav Airlines DC-9 on its way from Stockholm to Belgrade. Croatian

terrorists, at war with Marshall Tito (who had put Croatia under Serb domination in the old Yugoslavia), planted a bomb aboard. The plane blew up over what is now the Czech Republic, and the 27 others aboard that flight all perished.

But Vulovic, by chance, was in the tail section of the plane, which fell to a snow-covered mountain slope and, instead of smashing to bits, took a life-saving bounce.

Vulovic's luck has become a benchmark: She is listed in *The Guinness Book of Records* for surviving the longest fall without a parachute. Her plane was flying at 33,330 feet when it exploded. She fell more than six miles and lived to tell about it.

"I've been lucky, because I haven't always been careful."

—*Robert Altman, filmmaker*

As Luck Would Have It

After landing a role in the movie *The Girl From Petrovka*, English actor Sir Anthony Hopkins scoured the bookstores of London, searching in vain for a copy of George Feifer's original 1971 novel. Then one day as he waited for a train in the Leicester Square underground station, he noticed a book lying discarded on a bench. It was *The Girl From Petrovka*.

Oddly enough, George Feifer had been looking for a copy of the book, too. His own copy. Two years earlier, he loaned it to a friend, who promptly lost it. When the movie's filming began in Vienna, Hopkins met Feifer, and told him the amazing story of how he'd come across a copy in Leicester Square. As Hopkins described the strange notations throughout, Feifer turned white.

Hopkins had found Feifer's book.

"It was not enough, Napoleon observed, that he should have good generals; he wanted them to be lucky generals, also. In foreign affairs brains, preparation, judgement and power are of utmost importance, but luck is essential."

—*Dean Acheson, former secretary of state, "Homage to Plain Dumb Luck,"* Esquire

Turquoise Luck

You've undoubtedly seen, and perhaps even own, a piece of beautifully worked turquoise and silver jewelry made by the Navajo. But did you know that since ancient times, turquoise has been considered one of the luckiest of all lucky stones?

In ancient folkways ranging around the world, turquoise has been thought to bestow good luck as well as physical health. (Sometimes it's hard to separate the two.) There's an old belief that if either your luck or your health are about to take a turn for the worse, the turquoise ring or necklace you're wearing will grow pale in color. (The solution: put away the faded stone and get a new one that's a brighter blue.)

A Persian manuscript written in the eleventh century explained that turquoise brings good luck because its name, in Persian, means "the victorious." Among the Pima Indians of southern Arizona, the luck-bestowing powers of turquoise were valued so highly that if someone lost a favorite stone, it was viewed as an ominous event, foreshadowing bad luck. A medicine man had to be called in to restore the lost luck (if not the lost stone).

In Tibet, turquoise is said to guard against the Evil Eye (malevolent influences). There the stone has taken on an almost sacred character, and is often used to adorn statues of the Buddha or other religious figures.

Reverence for the lucky sea-blue stones dates all the way back to the early dynasties of ancient Egypt. In one famous old tale from those long-gone days, the reigning pharaoh, in order to relieve a fit of depression, takes a pleasure trip on the palace lake in a boat rowed by twenty beautiful, richly attired maidens. While bending over the oar, one of the maidens drops a particularly beautiful turquoise-encrusted hair comb into the water. Both she and the pharaoh are horrified. But—presto!—the court magician Zazamankh, who's also riding in the boat, comes to the rescue with a magical chant that causes the lost turquoise to float to the surface of the water like a cork. The maiden, snatching up the comb, is overjoyed.

Her turquoise—and her good luck—have returned.

"Chance is perhaps the pseudonym of God when He did not wish to sign."

—*Anatole France*

"In the queer mess of human destiny the determining factor is Luck. For every important place in life there are many men of fairly equal capacities. Among them Luck decides who shall accomplish the great work, who shall be crowned with laurel, and who shall fall back into silence and obscurity."

—*William E. Woodward*

"As I get older and more experienced, I realize more and more that luck in itself is neither good nor bad. Luck is raw magical energy. It is up to us to rally our skill, our presence of mind and knowhow, and claim it as knowledge and power. That is what is meant by 'good luck.'"

—Harlan Thornton, in a post to the Internet discussion group about luck, luckiness, lucky objects, amulets, and rituals

RALPH TOWNSEND (WHO WANTS TO WIN THE TEXAS LOTTERY A SECOND TIME):
"I believe in God, and I believe things can happen by prayer."

OPRAH WINFREY:
"Uh-huh. Do you think God wants you to win another $19.4 million?"

RALPH TOWNSEND:
"Probably not."

OPRAH WINFREY (TO AUDIENCE):
"He's trying to push God a little bit."

—The Oprah Winfrey Show

"It is a very bad thing to become ac- customed to good luck."

—*Publilius Syrus*

"Men live at the mercy of forces they cannot control. Belief in fortune and luck, good and evil, is one of the most widespread and persistent of human beliefs. Chance has been deified by many peoples. Fate has been set up as an overlord to whom even the Gods must bow. Belief in a Goddess of Luck is in ill repute among pious folk, but their belief in providence is a tribute to the fact no individual controls his own destiny."

—*John Dewey*

Good Luck on Campus . . .

Most college professors pooh-pooh superstition as ignorant quackery. Meanwhile, most college students will happily seize upon any good-luck charm or ritual that might give their grades a boost. It's so commonplace that many schools have a communal superstition. Here are a few of the more venerable good-luck traditions on campus.

At Bryn Mawr College, students seeking good luck at exam time go skinny-dipping in the cloister fountain at the Thomas library. The tradition dates back to Katharine Hepburn, who graduated in 1928. Another tradition is to make offerings to the library's plaster statue of Athena. During finals week she's decked out with flower garlands, streamers, candles, cards, notes, and poems.

At Iowa State, there's a raised bronze zodiac on the floor just inside the north entrance to the student union. Everyone walks around it—because if you step on it, you'll flunk your next exam. The only way to break the curse is to throw a penny off the bridge at the bottom of Union Hill.

At Roanoke College, a Lutheran school in Salem, Virginia, a concrete post was placed near Trout Hall back in the 1920s to block traffic. Now it's called "The Kicking Post" because students kick it for good luck.

Bryant College, a business school in Smithfield, Rhode Island, was founded more than a century ago in nearby Providence. When the school moved to its current location in 1971, an iron gate was relocated to the new campus as a memento of the school's roots. But it became, instead, a bad-luck charm. Students believed that if they walked through the gate, they'd flunk out! So many students avoided it that a brick path had to be built—around the gate. But it's good luck to finally "walk through the Archway" on your way to graduation ceremonies.

At Williams College in western Massachusetts, every commencement since 1916 has included the ceremonial dropping of a watch off the 80-foot spire of the college chapel. If it breaks, the graduating class will have good luck.

At the University of the South in Sewanee, Tennessee, the good-luck tradition is to touch the ceiling of your car as you leave the school gates. By doing this, you take your guardian angel with you to the outside world. When you come back, you touch the ceiling again to release your guardian angel—because you're safely back on campus.

More School Traditions

By far the most common good-luck tradition at college is rubbing the nose—or some other part of the anatomy—of a prominent statue. For example:

At Harvard, students rub the left foot of the statue of John Harvard, who sits outside University Hall in Harvard Yard.

At Cal Tech in Los Angeles, a statue of Robert Milliken, the noted physicist and former Cal Tech president, has a shiny nose from all the kids hoping to pass their physics exams.

In the lobby of Dartmouth's Hopkins Center, students shine the nose of a bust of Warner Bentley, a past director of the center, which is the school's arts complex. And at Brown, the shiny nose on campus belongs to the statue of John Hay at the John Hay Library.

At Marist College in Poughkeepsie, New York, a six-foot statue of Blessed Marcellin Champagnat, founder of the Marist order, faces the school's chapel. Father Champagnat's right arm is extended downward, palm up. Come exam time, students give him a "low five."

At Texas Christian University, students touch the nose of a statue of the school mascot, a horned frog, as they pass by on their way to exams.

At Northeastern University in Boston, the mascot is King Husky, a bronze statue outside Blackman Auditorium, which is the customary site of exams for all those huge, 101-level classes. Everyone rubs the sled dog's nose on their way in.

At nearby Tufts, generations of students rubbed the trunk of Jumbo, a stuffed elephant on display in the

Barnum Museum, which contained donations from the legendary circus entrepreneur. Since the original Jumbo was destroyed by a fire, today's students rub the trunk of his stone successor, Jumbo II.

At the University of Maryland at College Park, the school mascot is a Maryland terrapin named Testudo. His statue sits in front of McKeldin Library, a gift of the Class of '33. According to legend, rubbing his nose before an exam brings good luck. Legend also has it that, if a virgin ever graduates from College Park, the bronze statue will rise up from its pedestal during commencement and fly over the crowd.

Supernatural Study Aids

Percentages of psychology students at Connecticut College reporting engaging in various exam-related superstitions:

62%	Used a lucky pen, piece of jewelry, or clothing
28%	Wore sloppy clothes (dressed down)
33%	Dressed up
36%	Touched a lucky object
54%	Sat in a particular seat
38%	Listened to special music or song before the exam
26%	Ate a particular food before the exam
23%	Avoided a particular person, place, or action
31%	Performed a lucky action or sequence of actions
13%	Used another luck-enhancing strategy (e.g., perfume)

—Stuart A. Vyse, Believing in Magic:
The Psychology of Superstition

"Believing in luck is believing that life is a series of opportunities that aren't necessarily there for the reasons you think they are. Like, if I missed an airplane flight; on the one hand I could say it screwed everything up—but on the other, maybe this happened for some reason, maybe on the next flight I'll meet someone it may be good for me to meet.

"Believing in it a little bit sometimes frees you up to not worry about things you can't control."

—*Jerilyn Ross, talk-show psychologist*

Lucky Genes

Some people are just luckier than others; no doubt about that. But what if their luck were an inborn trait, like long legs or hazel eyes? Imagine that—and then imagine a strain of humanity that was bred for luck. Imagine the luckiest people on earth having children, and so on for hundreds of years . . .

That's the premise of a 1970 science-fiction novel titled *Ringworld.* Far into the future, the human race enacts strict fertility laws to maintain a sustainable population on the planet. An alien race of superior beings on a distant world takes notice, and decides to meddle with the situation in order to perform a truly cosmic genetics experiment. Working behind the scenes, they cause a crisis with the existing laws, then subtly manipulate the outcome: a New Year's Day lottery, each year, in which people win the right to have children by taking part in a global lottery. The consequence of such a system is that brute strength or brains or beauty no longer provides a winning evolutionary edge. Survival of the fittest no longer applies. It's literally the survival of the luckiest.

"Your species has been incredibly lucky," says an alien to a human midway through the novel, in explaining why his race chose to interfere. "Your history reads like a series of hair-breadth escapes, from intraspecies atomic war, from pollution of your planet with industrial wastes, from ecological upsets, from dangerously massive asteroids, and even from the core explosion, which you discovered only by the merest accident.

"And so we changed the Fertility Laws of Earth. . . . We were able to introduce the Birthright Lotteries. We hoped to produce a strain of unusually lucky humans."

And they did—but to go on would give away the ending.

The
Library Angels

What causes good luck? When it happens, does it mean anything? Is it something other than sheer happenstance? The British novelist Arthur Koestler (author of *Darkness at Noon*) believed that coincidences were not always "just a coincidence." In his later works, *The Roots of Coincidence* and *The Challenge of Chance*, he took the measure of various parapsychology experiments and concluded that the modern western concepts of chance and randomness were basically flawed. He urged readers to be open-minded about an "unknown principle operating beyond physical causality."

He collected anecdotes of meaningful coincidences and—not surprisingly, since he knew most of the European intellectuals of the mid-20th century—many anecdotes centered on library research. A standout example was from Dame Rebecca West, who was looking up material related to a man accused at the Nuremburg trials. In a letter to Koestler she described how the trial transcripts were collected into volumes that filled shelf upon library shelf—and the index was nearly useless. After hours of fruitless searching, she complained to the librarian, "I can't find it, there's no clue, it may be in any one of these volumes." She then put out her hand, grabbed a volume apparently at random, and opened it. She'd not only found the right volume, but the right page.

A second anecdote was from a man whose dying father left him . . . an unfinished scholarly work to complete! Some of the footnotes were incomplete, and he had to fill in exact page references. He polished off all of them except for one, which came from somewhere in a 36-volume work. He sat down with three of the most likely volumes, said a "sort of prayer," picked up one of the three books—and opened it to the exact place.

"After reading through a score of 'library cases'," Koestler wrote in *The Challenge of Chance*, "one is tempted to think of library angels in charge of providing cross references."

"Meaningful coincidences are manifestations of an all-embracing universal order."

—*Arthur Koestler,*
The Roots Of Coincidence

"Luck has nothing to do either with ratios or morals: It is in essence something magical . . . The ingenious lucky man, endowed with gifts by good fairies, the darling of the gods, is no subject for rational observations on the part of his biographers, and stands outside the personal and the historical."

—*Hermann Hesse,* Magister Ludi

Winston Churchill's Great Escape

When Winston Churchill was not yet 25 years old and had already lost his first parliamentary election, he signed on as a correspondent for the *London Morning Post*. His assignment: the Boer War, in which Britain fought the Dutch colonists of South Africa for control of its fabled gold and diamond mines. Little did he know it would earn him instant fame in his homeland.

He was riding with British troops on an armored train when it was ambushed by Boer raiders. Captured, he was marched off to a prisoner-of-war camp in Pretoria. The prison was a long tin dormitory enclosed by a corrugated iron fence topped with barbed wire, watched by armed guards 50 yards apart, and lit by searchlights at night.

Churchill was in this prison for less than a month when he heard of an escape plan hatched by two fellow prisoners. The plan was simple: jump the fence by the toilet at the rear of the enclosure, which was shielded from the searchlights. He insisted on going along. So on a Tuesday night, December 12, 1899, Churchill went to the latrine. Seeing the guard turn to light his pipe, Churchill saw his chance and leapt over the wall. In the garden on the other side, he crouched and waited for the others. But they were luckless; the guard wouldn't take his eyes—or his rifle—off them. Suddenly he was in this alone: a young man in a foreign land who didn't know the language, didn't have a compass or a map, and was a good three hundred miles away from friendly territory. Without a prayer, he walked out into the moonlit evening.

That night he hiked until he came upon a railroad track, jumped aboard the next train, crawled beneath a pile of empty coal bags, and fell asleep. Awaking again before dawn, he jumped off. Once the sun rose, he thought he'd found his luck: the tracks headed east, into the sun, and eventually into Portuguese East Africa and freedom.

But his great escape was not to be so easy. He hid during the day, hoping to jump an eastbound train under cover of darkness. No train came; fearing pursuit, he began walking east. That didn't work: Every bridge was guarded by armed Boers, and he had to cut a wide swath around them. At the next railroad station he nearly jumped aboard another train, but was scared off by voices. And so, in desperation, he wandered off, exhausted and aimless, to cross the vast South African plain.

At length he saw the fires of a native village. His only hope was to find a native who could be bribed. He chose a house at random and knocked. A tall, pale man holding a revolver opened the door and asked, in English, "What do you want?" When Churchill told him who he was, the man pulled him inside, thrust out his hand, and said, "Thank God you have come here! It is the only house for twenty miles where you would not have been handed over." He was 75 miles away from his POW camp, totally lost—and he knocked on the right door.

The four inhabitants were British miners. They gave him a bottle of whiskey and a leg of mutton and hid him at the bottom of a coal mine for three days; eventually he was spirited aboard a train heading to Portuguese East Africa. He hid under bales of wool while another Englishman, a local shipping agent, rode along on the train and distracted Boer soldiers with bribes and drinks until they reached the border. (By then, "Wanted" posters of Churchill were everywhere, and a price had been put on his head.)

When the train finally reached the port of Lourenço Marques, Churchill popped out from under the wool bales and, out of sheer joy, fired his pistol into the air. He walked off into the town, turned a couple of corners, and saw, on the roof of the building opposite, a Union Jack flying. It was the British Consulate. Churchill was safe. More than that, he was a national hero.

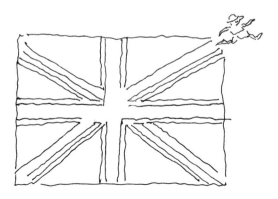

"The sun once stood still; the Wheel of Fortune, never!"

—*Spanish proverb*

"Good luck is what is left over after intelligence and efforts have combined at their best . . . Luck is the residue of design."

—*Branch Rickey, the innovative baseball manager who hired Jackie Robinson and invented the farm team system*

Left to Right Is Right

One of Winston Churchill's biographers, Walter Graebner, noted that in his daily life this eminent 20th-century statesman was quite superstitious. "At the very beginning of the meal, almost before anyone had pulled his chair in, a bottle of well-chilled champagne would be placed in front of Mr. Churchill," Graebner recalled, "and Churchill always poured for everyone within reach. Then he would pass the bottle along and ask the others to help themselves. He took great care to see that the bottle was always passed to the left."

Passing to the left is good luck (and passing to the right is bad luck) because the sun travels from left to right. In the high northern latitudes of Europe, the sun travels low in the southern sky—especially in winter. So if you face south, you're facing the sun, and from that aspect the sun crosses the sky from left to right. Performing a task from left to right puts you in sync with the sun's diurnal rhythm and its life-giving power. When you pass to the left, the champagne travels from left to right (in front of you) around the table; it starts with the person on your left, and completes the circle with the person on your right.

The Lucky Hat That
Won the Gold

Some men believe they have a "lucky hat" that brings them good luck. The most famous lucky hat in recent memory was a battered white golf cap worn by Dave Wottle in the 1972 Olympics.

Wottle was a 21-year-old ROTC student at Bowling Green University in Ohio when he ran the Olympic trials early that summer. He entered as a strong contender in the 1500-meter run (roughly a mile). As a lark, he decided to try out for the 800-meter event; he thought it would be more fun than running yet another practice session of the 1500. But he didn't hold out much hope for himself: "I'm no half-miler," he told reporters before the trial. "I run stupid races. I don't have any idea what I'm doing."

He did well enough to qualify for the 800-

meter Olympic race that September in Munich. He wasn't given much chance of winning. As the race got underway, Wottle seemed to be living down to everybody's expectations: he ran dead last for 500 meters. Then he suddenly picked up speed, passed two Kenyans on the outside, and took aim at the Russian favorite in the lead. In the final moments, he lunged for the finish line, and beat the flagging Russian—by the length of his lucky cap!

Yes, he wore his lucky cap in an Olympic race. It was so much a part of him, it created a famous little stir afterward—he forgot to take it off when they played the national anthem.

A Banner Year

When Frank Viola was a left–handed pitcher for the Minnesota Twins back in 1984, he looked up into the stands one day to see a huge banner: "FRANKIE SWEET MUSIC VIOLA." It had been hung by a young fan named Mark Dornfeld. Dornfeld started bringing his banner to games on a fairly steady basis. Over the course of the next two seasons, Viola noticed that he never lost a game when the banner was on display.

Finally, in 1987, Dornfeld met Viola. They talked. And Viola continued to win. By the end of the regular season, Viola was 15-0 in banner games—and the Twins were headed for the World Series.

When Viola found out that Dornfeld didn't have a ticket for Game 1, his wife Kathy called up Dornfeld to offer hers.

Dornfeld was there, with his banner, to watch Viola pitch. Viola won the game. The series went to seven games, and in that final game, Viola was called to pitch again. Dornfeld was there, the banner was there—and Viola won! The Twins were the champions of baseball, and Frankie "Sweet Music" Viola was named Series MVP.

Jinxing the Evil Eye

In the fall of 1996, the San Jose State University football team launched a bizarre public search for a woman named Josephine Canicatti, now 83, who is supposed to have cost the Yankees the 1955 World Series by casting her "evil eye" on Casey Stengel.

They just wanted to use her services to put a jinx on the opposition.

Is there really any such thing as the "evil eye"? Well, we can't say for sure. But the reason we mention it is that belief in the evil eye is one of the most ancient and widespread superstitions in the world. And most good-luck charms were originally meant as shields against it.

The whole idea seems to have grown out of a basic human suspicion: That it's bad luck to brag too loudly when things are going great, else your boasting may attract

jealous and perhaps even malicious attention. After all, it's only natural to secretly
despise somebody who's doing well, especially if they're all puffed up about it.
There's a related, more ancient idea that
magical forces or rays emanate from the
human body, and the most potent rays
come from the eyes. Beautiful, enviable
things like handsome children or great
riches are thought to be especially prone to
attracting these malevolent rays.

On the other hand, strangely enough,
people also believed that having the evil eye
didn't necessarily mean you meant somebody harm. You could have the evil eye
without even knowing it, potentially harm-
ing someone you loved or even yourself. In
1889, an Italian writer named Guiseppe
Pitre reported that there was a man in
Messina "whose glance was considered so
fatal that at his death the rumor spread that
he died because . . . he just happened to

look in a large mirror displayed in a store window."

But by carrying a good-luck charm or performing a good-luck ritual, people came to believe you could deflect or distract the evil eye.

That's why we "knock on wood" after crowing about how well things are going. That's why a Hindu mother will complain that her child is wasting away, ugly, and unhealthy. It's not because the infant actually is but because to lavishly praise the child is bad luck, and an invitation to the evil eye.

These ideas are so old they're embedded in the English language. For instance, in ancient times Roman generals would parade in front of crowds after great military victories. But because they'd then placed themselves squarely in the gaze of thousands of people, they were especially vulnerable to the evil eye. In order to deflect it, they began mounting on the front of their chariots the image of an obscene god named Fascinus. From that indecent Roman god came the English word "fascinate," which originally meant to bewitch by the evil eye.

Some good-luck charms were protection against the evil eye because they themselves had the evil eye. Rabbits were widely believed to have the evil eye, which is part of the reason why a rabbit's foot has long been considered good luck. It's a sort of "countercharm" against the evil eye.

Now, we're not here to tell you that it will do any good if San Jose State can actually find the lady who "jinxed" Casey Stengel. We're just here to say that these ancient traditions about luck contain some deep, useful human wisdom.

As Yale sociologist William Graham Sumner put it in a classic book called *Folk-*

ways: "It follows from the notion of the evil eye that men should never admire, praise, congratulate or encourage those who are rich, successful, prosperous and lucky. The right thing to do is to . . . scoff at them in their prosperity. That may offset their good luck, check their pride, and humble them a little."

Which isn't bad advice—especially if they want to stay lucky.

"Wanting something intensely is the motivating power that produces good luck."

—*Bernard Gittelson,* How to Make Your Own Luck

The Gypsy Robe of Broadway

Come opening night on Broadway, the cast members of every musical take part in an elaborate luck-giving ritual. Well before curtain time the show's performers gather in a circle on the stage. Most of them belong to the chorus of dancers and singers—gypsies, they're called in the theater business. One of them will be awarded the Gypsy Robe.

The giving of the Gypsy Robe goes back five decades, when a chorus member of the 1950 production of *Gentlemen Prefer Blondes* sent a dressing gown to a friend—another gypsy—who was appearing in *Call Me Madam.* On it was pinned a cabbage rose from Ethel Merman's costume. It was given as a private token of good luck—but the recipient added a memento from *Call Me Madam* and sent it on to a gypsy in another show just opening. And a ritual was born.

The original robe is long gone. In fact, each Gypsy Robe has to be replaced after 20 shows or so because by then it's chock full of lucky charms (usually scraps of costume with show logos). Then a new one is started. And on opening night, it's delivered to the theater by a gypsy who wore it at the last Broadway opening.

That gypsy steps into the circle on stage to award the robe to the gypsy in the cast who has appeared in the greatest number of Broadway shows. There is total silence. The winner's name is announced; everyone screams, claps, and cries. The new owner puts on the robe and parades three times around the circle as cast members touch it for good luck. The new owner must then visit all the dressing rooms, spreading more luck. It's an hour until showtime; they've already summoned all their talent, energy, and experience. What they need now is a charm.

"I'm a great believer in luck. I find myself instantly liking people who credit their success to a lucky break."

—*Robert Venturi,* Architect

Was It a Good Year?

The Romans had a custom of throwing different colored stones into an urn every day—a white stone if they'd had a lucky day, a black one if they'd been unlucky. At the end of the year, they added up the stones to figure out if it had been a lucky year or an unlucky one.

The race is not to the swift, nor the battle to the strong, nor bread to the wise, nor riches to the intelligent . . . but time and chance happen to them all.

—*Ecclesiastes 9:11*

Regarding Rings

✤ If you wear a ring on your thumb it will
  bring good luck.

✤ A ring baked in a cake brings a lover to the
  one who finds it.

✤ Changing the rings on your fingers will
  change your luck.

A Dropped Eyelash

If one of your eyelashes drops out, and you find it, you have a rare chance to make a wish come true. Place it on the back of your left hand, then smack your left hand from underneath, on the palm, with the back of your right hand. If it flies off by the third try, then it has gone off somewhere to bring back your wish. Or so you hope . . .

Our Favorite Luck Lore from the Pennsylvania Dutch

- ❖ It's good luck to kiss in the middle of a covered bridge.

- ❖ If a woman is getting anxious to marry, she should start feeding a cat from her shoe.

- ❖ If a man is spurned by a woman, he can change his luck by crawling three times under a briar which has taken second root.

- ❖ Name a son Adam, and the next child will be a girl.

- ❖ Eating anything that has grown double will cause twins.

- ❖ Children born on Christmas can hear and understand "cattle talk."

- ❖ Burn a baby's first diaper for good luck.

- ❖ Paying the doctor in full will stunt a child's growth.

✣ If a child develops whooping cough, put a
 live trout in the child's mouth, let the child
 breathe three times, then put the trout
 back in the stream while it's still alive.

✣ If you eat the last piece of bread, you'll become an old maid.

"An ounce of luck is better than a pound of wisdom."

—*Italian proverb*

"Luck is not faith, but fun in the face of the absurdities of life."

—*Wayne E. Oates,* Luck:
A Secular Faith

More Time-Honored Ways to Improve Your Luck

1. Keep a crooked coin in a left-side pocket, in your purse—or under your pillow for nine nights.

2. Hide a lucky bean and don't let anyone know where it is.

3. Trim your fingernails Monday morning before breakfast.

4. Sprinkle a little nutmeg on your lottery tickets.

5. Give a poor person a pair of new shoes.

6. Put money in the pockets of a new suit before wearing it—and they'll never be empty.

7. Before sleep, place your shoes with the toes pointing under the bed.

"I'm a lucky man, Horace, a lucky man. To dream and to live to get what you've dreamed of. That's my idea of a lucky man."

—*Lillian Hellman's* The Little Foxes

Luck in the New Year

In Bolivia, people eat 12 grapes at the stroke of midnight. In Greece, a loaf of bread is baked with a coin in it somewhere— and the person who gets the slice with the coin will be lucky all year. In North Carolina, people used to eat black-eyed peas at midnight.

All over the world, people believe that if they perform the right little ceremony at New Year, they'll be lucky all year. In Scotland, for example, the "first foot" custom decrees that the first foot over the threshhold decides the luck for the year. So at midnight on New Year, a dark-haired man should come in the front door with a lump of coal, a coin, and a bit of bread (or a bottle of whisky) . . . symbols of money, food, and warmth.

Many American immigrants brought their traditional New Year customs with them. In Pennsylvania, folks of German heritage (the Pennsylvania "Dutch") eat sauerkraut on New Year's Day for a prosperous coming year. In the Appalachians, eating collard greens will bring paper money all year. People in the Ozarks filled their saltshakers, and in Louisiana the Creole custom is to wear something new on New Year's.

With the New Year, new hope.

"My luck is getting worse and worse. Last night, for instance, I was mugged by a Quaker."

—*Woody Allen*

How the Chinese Give Good Luck

The Chinese New Year is a time when everybody calls on friends and relatives to exchange good luck. Tea and sweets are ceremoniously offered to each guest, the sweets being offered on a special octagonal tray. The guest will take some sweets, and in return place in the tray's center a little present of silver coins wrapped in red paper. This package is sometimes known as *lay shee* ("good-luck piece"). Red is a lucky color in China; its symbolism goes back to blood and flame, the sources of life.

Lay shee or *hong bao* is given by married and older people to unmarried people and children—but it is, in a way, an exchange. The older people, in giving good luck, are getting some in return. They believe the vitality of the young people will help them.

"Yes, I am very lucky, but I have a little theory about this. I have noticed through experience and observation that providence, nature, God, or what I would call the power of creation seems to favor human beings who accept and love life unconditionally . . ."

—*Arthur Rubinstein,* My Young Years

"When you have good luck in any-thing, you ought to be glad. Indeed, if you are not glad, you are not really lucky."

—*Henry Van Dyke,* Fisherman's Luck